This book is for my great friend Gary Kornblau,
the Magus of Art Issues. Magazine (1989–2001) —
the stage upon which we did our little dance

BEAU MONDE: TOWARD A REDEEMED COSMOPOLITANISM
SITE SANTA FE'S FOURTH INTERNATIONAL BIENNIAL

JULY 14, 2001—JANUARY 6, 2002 CURATED BY DAVE HICKEY

Beau Monde: Toward a Redeemed Cosmopolitanism

Gajin Fujita with Alex Kizu & Jessie Simon

Kenneth Anger
Sarah Morris
Nic Nicosia
Stephen Prina
Ed Ruscha
Jane & Louise Wilson

Jeff Burton

Takashi
Murakami

Ellsworth Kelly

Gajin Fujita

Ken Price

Jessica
Stockholder

Marine
Hugonnier

Kermit Oliver

Jo Baer

Pia Fries

Jim Isermann

Darryl
Montana

Frederick
Hammersley

James Lee Byars

Bridget
Riley

Jorge
Pardo

Jesús Rafael Soto

Josiah
McElheny

Alexis Smith

Jennifer Steinkamp & Jimmy Johnson

Graft Design

Participating Artists

Kenneth Anger

Jo Baer

Jeff Burton

James Lee Byars

Pia Fries

Gajin Fujita

Graft Design

Frederick Hammersley

Marine Hugonnier

Jim Isermann

Ellsworth Kelly

Josiah McElheny

Darryl Montana

Sarah Morris

Takashi Murakami

Nic Nicosia

Kermit Oliver

Jorge Pardo

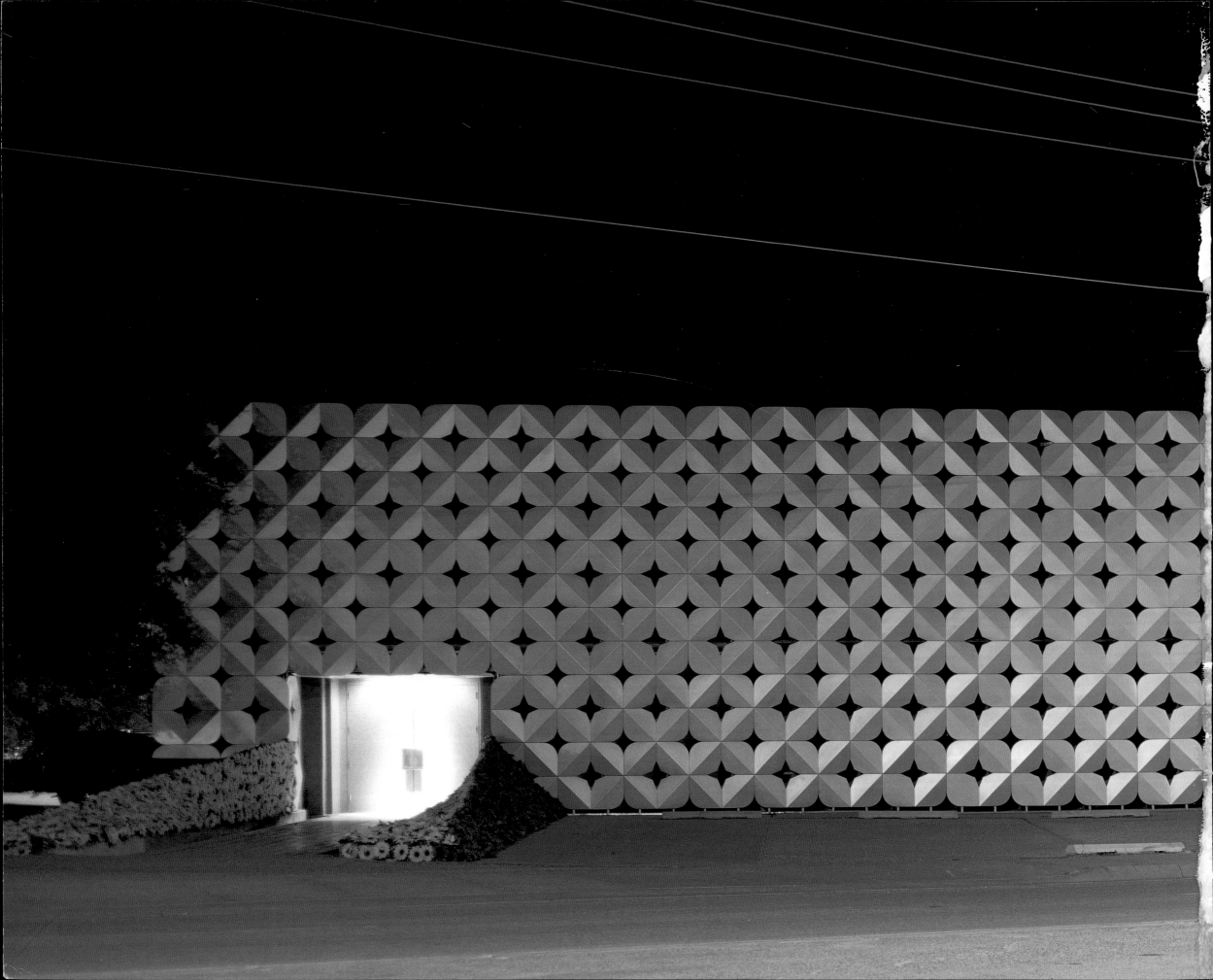

SITE *Santa Fe*

LOUIS GRACHOS, Director

SITE SANTA FE'S FOURTH INTERNATIONAL BIENNIAL, *Beau Monde: Toward a Redeemed Cosmopolitanism*, marks yet another milestone in our commitment to presenting significant international exhibitions. The choice of renowned art critic and writer Dave Hickey as curator of the 2001 biennial is representative of SITE Santa Fe's mission to give independent curators the freedom to present unique international exhibitions within the context of our museum — site-specific projects that may be difficult to execute in larger art institutions.

This commitment began in 1995 with *Longing and Belonging: From the Faraway Nearby*, when Bruce Ferguson addressed issues concerning the individual, identity, and place in his biennial; and was continued in 1997's *Truce: Echoes of Art in an Age of Endless Conclusions*, in which Francesco Bonami used the biennial format as a context for considering global tensions and their impact on culture at large. In 1999's *Looking for a Place*, curated by Rosa Martínez, artists considered the meaning of place, focusing on how "universes" could be created anywhere in the world. *Looking for a Place* expanded the parameters of SITE Santa Fe's biennial exhibition format by making considerable use of off-site venues for various artists' projects. These previous three biennials were primarily governed, as many international exhibitions are, by political and social themes.

In this fourth international biennial, the focus is quite different, featuring, above all else, the pure pleasure of aesthetics, art, and design. Dave Hickey, who is a professor of Art Criticism and Theory at the University of Las Vegas in Nevada, a freelance writer for national and international publications, the author of three books (*The Invisible Dragon: Four Essays on Beauty, Air Guitar: Essays on Art and Democracy*, and *Stardumb*), and the recipient of a 2001 MacArthur Fellowship, is a seminal thinker in the world of art and cultural criticism. As a critic first and foremost, Hickey's vision for this biennial — one brought to fruition with the assistance of the Los Angeles-and Berlin-based architectural design firm Graft Design —

was to upturn the more traditional notions of international exhibitions as arenas for political or social agendas in which curators rather than a broader audience are engaged.

For *Beau Monde: Toward a Redeemed Cosmopolitanism*, Hickey initially sought to create an exhibition that is as much about the pleasure of looking at art and the viewers' experience of art within highly specific spaces, as it is about any other agenda. While intergenerational and intercultural influences became readily apparent in the exhibition's presentation, Hickey's emphasis was on beauty—that often forgotten but integral aspect of art. As Peter Schjeldahl notes in his review of *Beau Monde* in *The New Yorker* (August 13, 2001), "The importance of pleasure in aesthetic experience is so simple and self-evident. How did we reach a point where a forthright assertion of that idea by an art show can seem like a stroke of genius?"

Hickey's biennial is a brilliant counterpoint to the accepted biennial format—not only for the unrelenting priority it gives to beauty and its focus on this curator's personal tastes, but also for the way in which Hickey and Graft Design completely redesigned S I T E Santa Fe's warehouse space. In fact, these alterations have the effect of obscuring S I T E Santa Fe as audiences have come to know it, and create instead an environment specifically for Hickey's vision. In many ways, *Beau Monde* is an exhibition that returns to curator-focused methodology of presentation: A clear vision is the starting point and the exhibition spaces are designed with this vision and specific artworks in mind.

The new spaces begin outside, where S I T E Santa Fe's adobe façade has been covered by Gajin Fujita's color-saturated mural portraying the *Beau Monde* logo, as well as a silvery, shimmering building skin, a site-specific installation by Jim Isermann. These two distinctly different works—the former emerging out of a compelling combination of Japanese painting, Japanese comics, and graffiti; the latter an echo of Op and Pop Art—emphasize the vast range of art and beauty encompassed by what Hickey refers to as his catholic tastes. The entryway to the museum has been redesigned by Graft Design: Before, concrete; after, a garden path filled with sunflowers and enhanced by sound. The previously cube-like interior is newly defined by curved walls and rounded archways. Sightlines produced by opening and restructuring walls provide numerous combinations and juxtapositions for viewing the art. The picture window inserted in the back wall as part of the exhibition design not only lightens the gallery spaces and offers a view onto the landscape and railroad tracks beyond the museum, but also has been incorporated into Jessica Stockholder's installation for the biennial.

The redesigned spaces evidence a merger of art, design, and architecture that accommodates the artwork and visitors alike. This is an environment for viewing art that allows for the interplay of a variety of elements, such as media and color, and many different forms of art, including sculpture, painting, photography, film, and installation work. And, it is an environment that reflects Hickey's investigation of beauty as it emerges from what he describes as "the global field of overlapping and interfused idiomatic expression—the virtuoso accommodation of one cultural idiom to another that constitutes the very definition of cosmopolitanism." Hickey's vision, while governed by his own preferences and therefore highly subjective, nonetheless provides viewers with the raw materials for a multitude of personal experiences of the art and exhibition.

S I T E Santa Fe is proud to have commissioned many of the pieces for this biennial, including new works by Graft Design, Jeff Burton, Gajin Fujita, Jim Isermann, Josiah McElheny, Takashi Murakami, Alexis Smith, Jennifer Steinkamp and Jimmy Johnson, and Jessica Stockholder. I would like to thank S I T E Santa Fe's Board of Directors for their dedication and support, which make it possible to present such a unique and ambitious exhibition. I am grateful to Dave Hickey for his vision, Jack Woody and Twelvetrees Publishers for the production of this catalogue, S I T E Santa Fe's permanent staff, and those who worked specifically on this biennial. S I T E Santa Fe is honored to have the opportunity to present *Beau Monde*, an exhibition that reminds us all—art professionals and art lovers alike—of art's essential power, which, at its core, has always had much to do with beauty.

HEAVEN FOR WEATHER. HELL FOR COMPANY.

HEAVEN FOR WEATHER. HELL FOR COMPANY.

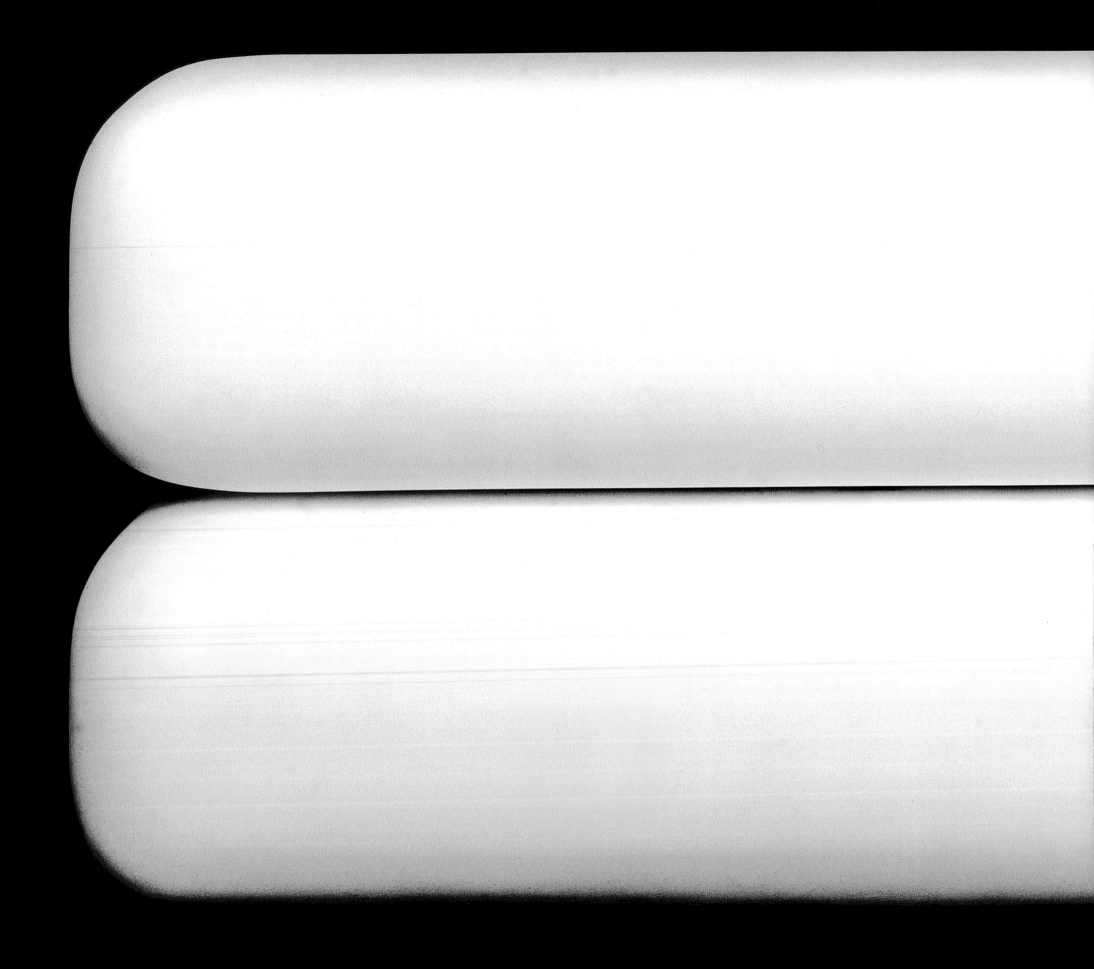

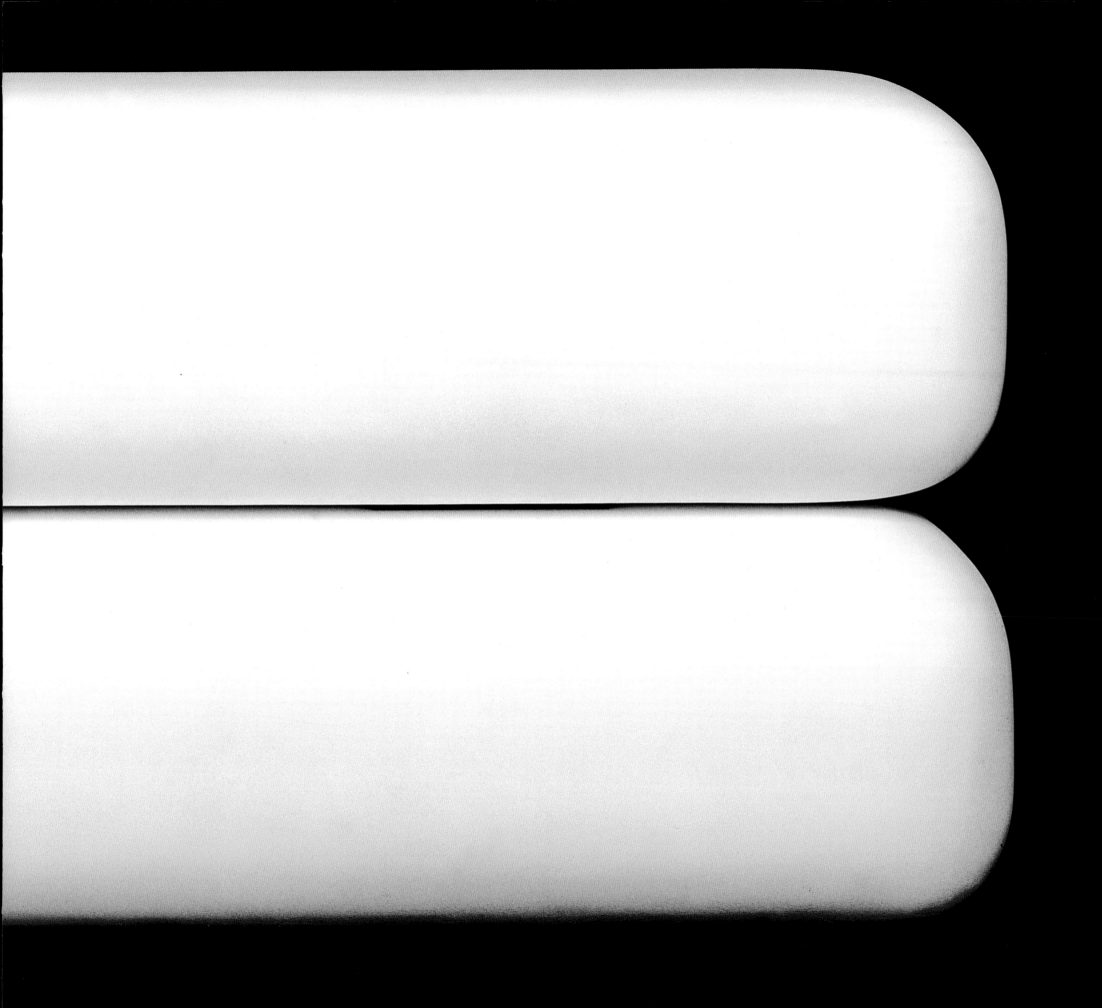

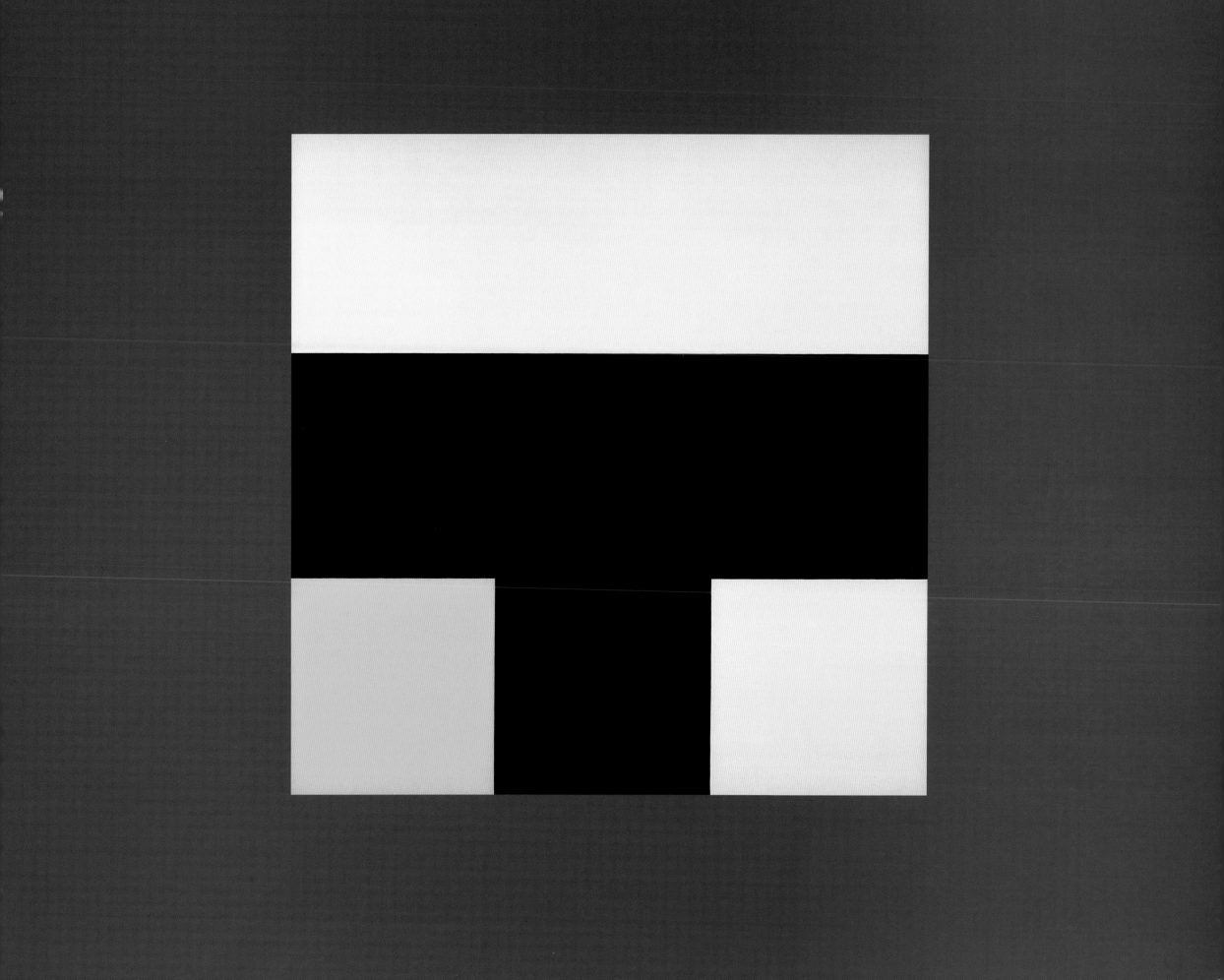

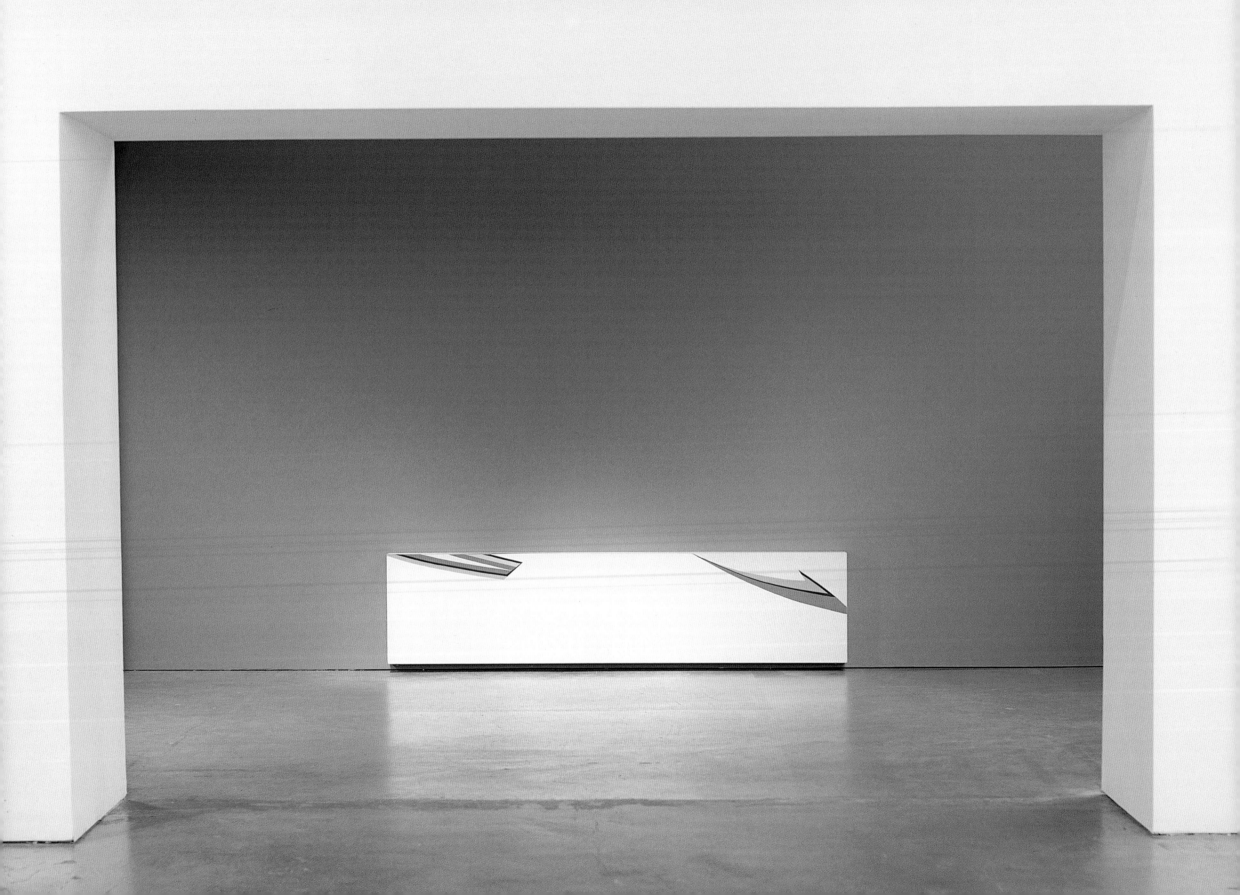

HEAVEN FOR WEATHER. HELL FOR COMPANY.

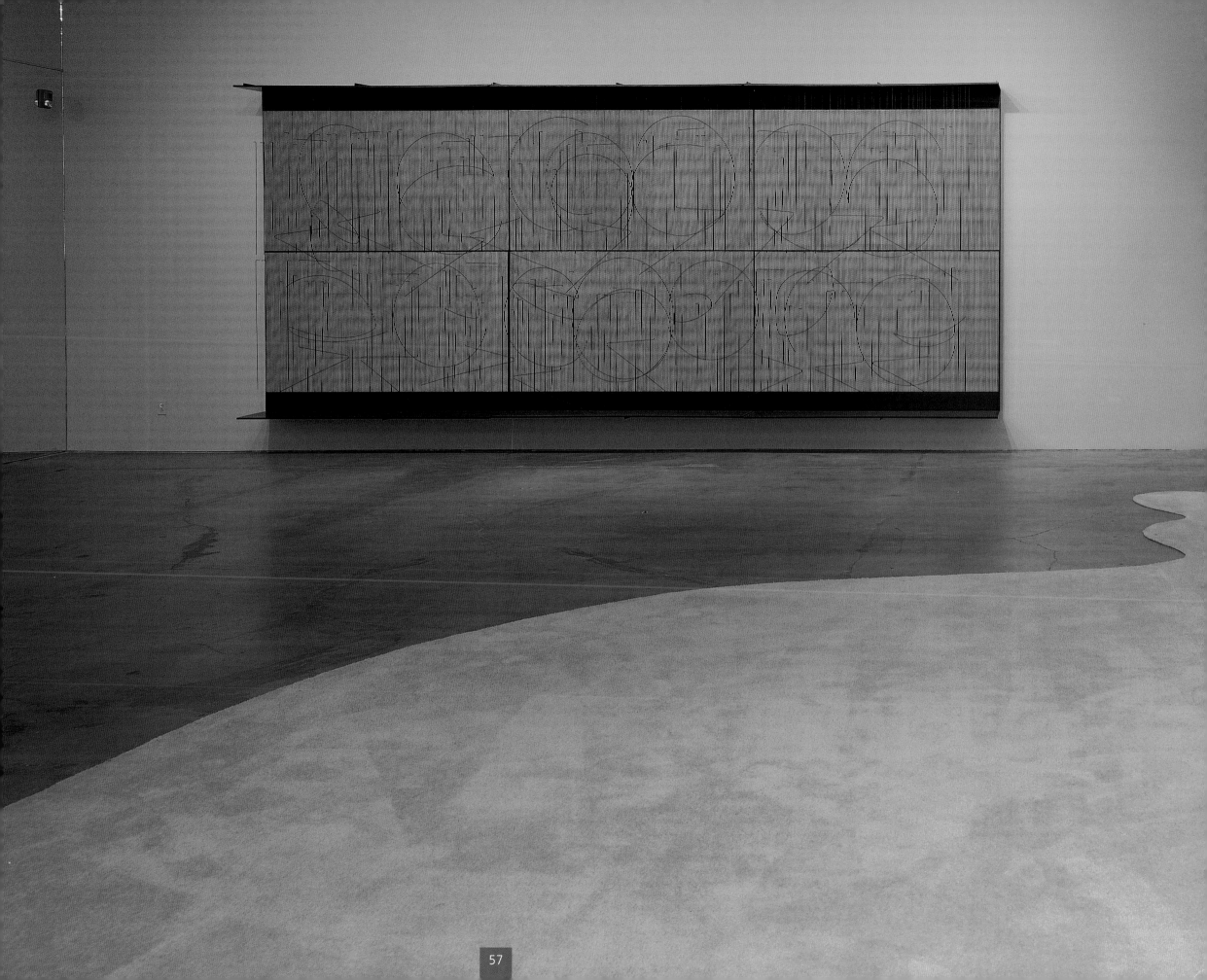

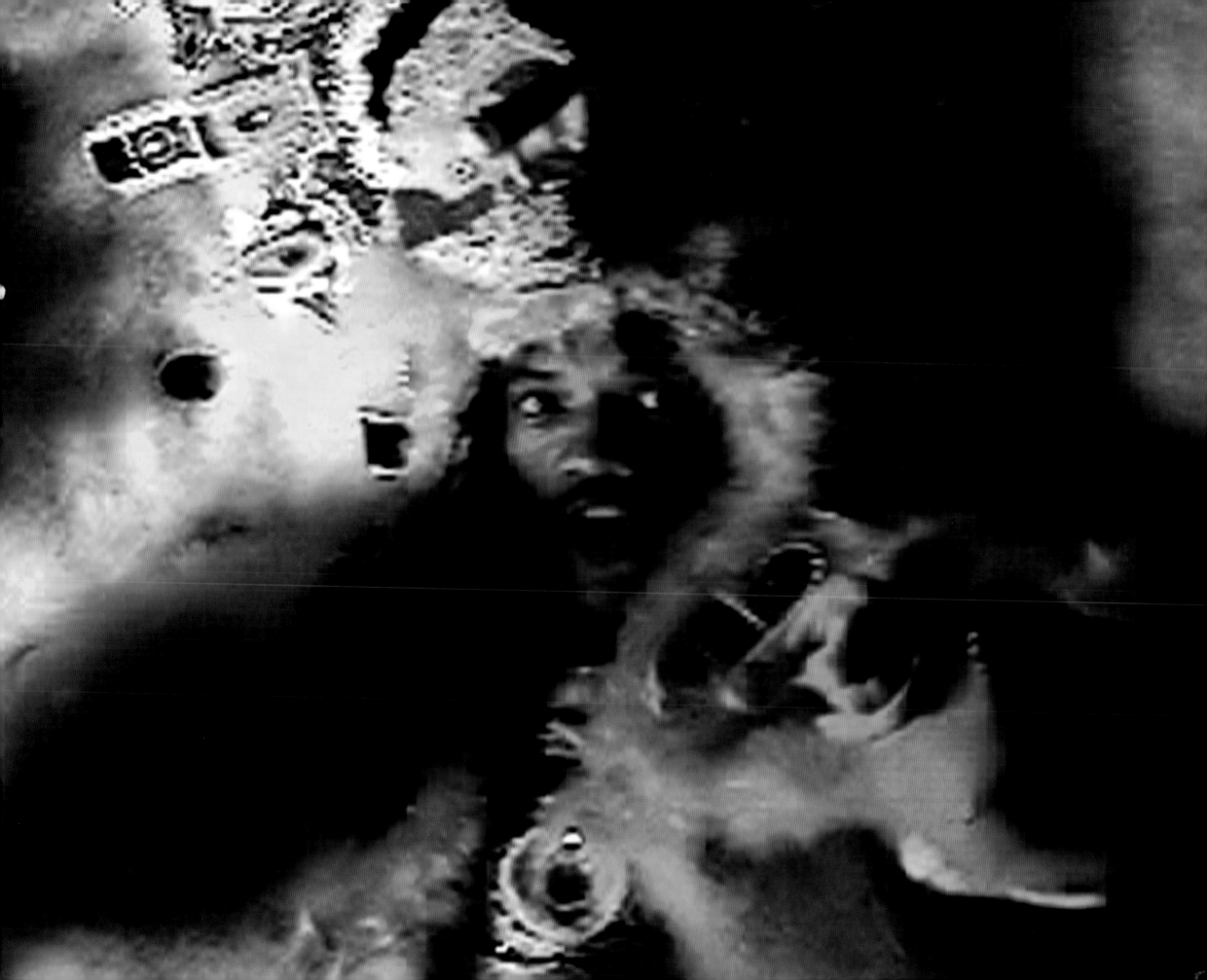

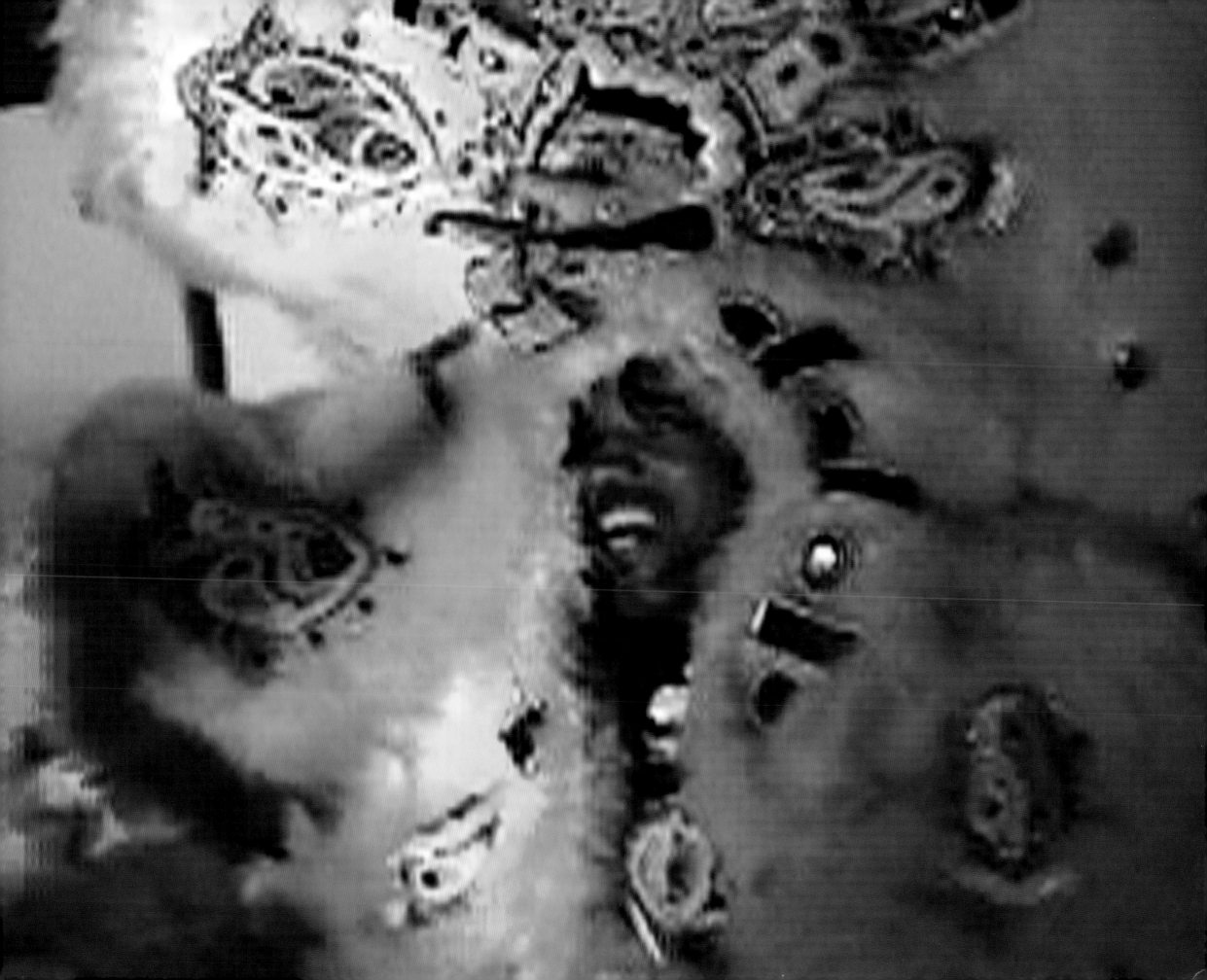

Beau Monde, Upon Reflection

DAVE HICKEY, Curator

TWO YEARS AGO, I accepted S I T E Santa Fe's invitation to curate an international biennial exhibition in New Mexico. It would have been cowardly not to accept, I thought, after 30 years of taking issue with other curators' exhibitions. Also, I wanted to do it. Criticism and curating are radically distinct activities, and I welcomed the change. Art critics toil on the consumer side of the art world, trying to make sense of what they are shown. Curators reign on the supply side, assembling works of art that other people might make sense of. As a long-time critic, I thought it would be fun, just once, to plan the big party rather than report on the guest list. I felt empowered to do so by the fact that exhibitions of serious art and critical essays about serious art do, in fact, have one thing in common: They are not themselves serious art. They are both highly conventionalized popular art forms. Like popular songs and residential architecture, art exhibitions are virtually identical in their parts, construction, and manner of address. Critical essays are equally similar. One differs from another only in refinement and detail. Whatever profundity they might aspire to, they derive from the serious art they engage.

Audiences for such works of popular art, then, have an experience that is only microscopically different from experiences they have had before. As a consequence, these audiences, inured by the conventions of the genre, are predisposed to overlook the subtle arguments and theoretical superstructures that inform such work. What they *will* take away from the experience, invariably, is the *tone* of the performance — the ambient atmosphere conveyed by the accumulation of small decisions. With this in mind, I resolved at the outset to concern myself as a curator with refinement and detail — to *touch everything* with high spirits and a light heart — and to let good art take care of the rest.

So, this is the way it went. I decided to call this exhibition *Beau Monde* for various reasons. First, because, many years ago, I wrote a book about beauty and have ever since been dubbed as the "beauty guy" by the popular press. It seemed best to beard this seedy lion in its den. Second, because the show was scheduled to open on Bastille Day, when the French celebrate the death of an antique *beau monde*. This seemed an appropriate birthday for a new *beau monde*. Finally, the expression, *beau monde* refers literally to a beautiful world and figuratively to an elite social milieu. Like any good democrat, I wished to conflate these meanings and create a beautiful, nonexclusionary social milieu—a *beau monde* generally, rather than *le beau monde* specifically. Also, I wished to comment obliquely on the international art world, which, at present, is a *beau monde* not much concerned with the *beaux-arts*.

In truth, I didn't think about it. *Beau Monde* seemed a high-spirited and lighthearted title. It felt right, so I picked it and moved on to the next rat's nest of details. All of the preceding "becauses," then, are after the fact, as are most of the "becauses" that follow. They amount to a teleological unpacking of cumulative decisions made quickly, in sequence, and on the spot. In practice, I tried to choose good works of art from all of the artists I selected. I selected 90 percent of these artists in five minutes on a Southwest Airlines flight from Las Vegas to Los Angeles, writing their names down on a yellow pad: my "dream team." The list was expressive of my own tastes, whims, intellectual concerns, tactical instincts, and art-historical consciousness at the moment. These are now embodied in the exhibition, and, even though sorting one reason out from another is blatantly artificial and probably irrelevant, I have tried to do a little sorting in the paragraphs that follow, simply because nothing comes from nowhere.

I can see in retrospect, for instance, that I instinctively chose to do a self-consciously "art historical" exhibition because it's what I know, because international exhibitions are art-historical occasions, and because most exhibitions of this sort are willfully disdainful of anything so parochial as art history. They aspire to a more totalizing "historical consciousness." As a practicing critic, I am congenitally skeptical of totalizing historical concepts, so I decided that in this exhibition I would momentarily abandon the quest for truth and strive for distinction—that, in short, I would try my very best not to be boring. Not being boring, thankfully, requires little in the way of totalizing historical consciousness, but it does require a modicum of art-historical awareness.

Igor Stravinsky always argued that an artist without tradition is doomed to plagiarism. What he meant by this, I think, is that, without some historical awareness, the precedents for what we do are indistinguishable from the art we practice. We know precedents whether we *know* that we know them or not, so unless we are acutely conscious of the accumulative tradition in which we work, unless we *learn* what we know, we plagiarize. Presented with the task of selecting an international exhibition in Santa Fe, New Mexico, I took Stravinsky's cautionary observation to heart. I began asking myself how, specifically, my own exhibition would distinguish itself from other international biennials, and how, specifically, my exhibition would distinguish itself from its site in Santa Fe. My answer to each of these questions turned out to be the same: I would privilege the cosmopolitan.

Over the years, international biennials have become quintessential cosmopolitan occasions perversely devoted to marketing ideas of regional identity and local exceptionality in the normative global language of post-minimalist artistic practice. Over a somewhat longer period, Santa Fe has evolved into a quintessential cosmopolitan vacation community that is also devoted to marketing fantasies of local exceptionality in the international iconography of contemporary resort culture. Both of these historical traditions presume that one place differs from another in its essence — in its essential content and circumstances — and that this essence can be communicated in an international language.

My quarrel with these rationales is twofold. First, the idea of global society as a collection of virtually autonomous provincial enclaves seems fantastical on its face. Second, the idea that the autonomous content of these provincial enclaves might be communicated in a single international idiom is at least equally risible. Also, this second idea contradicts the first — positing, as it does, some Platonic, international community of "understanding." The cautionary historical residue of this second proposition — the idea of a "global style" — was demonstrated for me in Robert Rosenblum's shrewd and elegant exhibition, *1900*, which opened at the Guggenheim Museum in New York in 2000. In *1900*, Rosenblum surveyed the last previous moment of international stylistic hegemony—the beginning of the twentieth century—when post-impressionism rather than post-minimalism was the dominant idiom.

What Rosenblum's exhibition made legible, at least to me, was the extent to which externally imposed styles deaden practice. On the walls of the Guggenheim, the crippling artifice of by-the-book Japanese and Scandinavian post-impressionism contrasted radically with French post-impressionism that freely appropriated from Japanese and Northern European sources. The lesson of this (which, of course, we already know) is that it is always safest to assume that places differ from one another not so much in the things that are done as in the *way* things are done. Style, then, is, irrevocably, cultural content.

As a curator, accepting this precept requires adopting a cosmopolitan rather than a global model of art practice. One must presume that, like politics and economics, all aesthetics are local, competitive, and impure—that art created in and for local venues acquires cosmopolitan attributes for local competitive advantage. This has been the case, I think, since Dürer went to Italy to become a better German artist; since Bassano cribbed the Germans for leverage in Venice; and, even today, outside the stylistic hegemony of institutional culture, this continues to be the case. In a cosmopolitan world of contiguous neighborhoods with porous boundaries, those neighborhoods whose artists and tradesmen most readily appropriate and adapt exotic attributes tend to predominate.

To take the case in point, the very richness of Santa Fe as a place derives from a stunning variety of cosmopolitan accommodations. Nothing, in fact, could be more eccentrically cosmopolitan than the area's porous and accommodating "spiritual climate," which allows Santa Fe to function peacefully as a kind of transcendental souk in which Catholics, Navajos, Buddhists, Sufis, Zunis, Baptists, Jews, Sikhs, vegans, and nuclear physicists vie for competitive spiritual advantage. "Santa Fe Style" itself derives from an unstable blend of romantic primitivism, native design, international-style modernism, and hacienda décor. (See Alexis Smith's installation in this exhibition.) Similar hybrids have prevailed in the great art centers of the late twentieth century. Far from manifesting autonomous integrity, the art produced in New York, Cologne, Tokyo, London, and Los Angeles during this period is defined by its acquisitive impurity. One may, of course, disapprove of this mongrelization on the grounds that it simultaneously subverts the autonomy of place, the autonomy of culture, and the autonomy of the artist. The hypocrisies inherent in espousing an internationally administered global provincialism, however, argue against doing so.

Through this thought process (much slowed down and gentrified by my description of it), it became obvious to me that I could honor my own interests and the tradition of international exhibitions (while distinguishing my exhibition from both its predecessors and its site) by simply emphasizing the suppressed *cosmopolitan* aspect of an international exhibition in Santa Fe. I could do this by prioritizing the impurity and complexity of both the occasion and the city rather than focusing on their separate, utopian aspirations to purity and simplicity. With this in mind, I set out to select works of art that visibly expressed the influence and confluence of diverse cultural resources.

In the beginning, I commissioned works by Alexis Smith and Jessica Stockholder that, in their interaction, would speak to the cosmopolitan aspects of culture in New Mexico. Then I embarked upon the selection of undeniably cosmopolitan works of art from around the world. I selected a British painting of French descent by Bridget Riley, an American painting by Ellsworth Kelly of similar provenance, a Japanese sculptural installation with sources in the Italian baroque by Takashi Murakami, a Venezuelan construction that declares its German and Russian precedents by Jesús Rafael Soto, two California paintings in a Dutch tradition by Frederick Hammersley, a German painting with American antecedents by Pia Fries, Creole costumes by Darryl Montana with precedents in the French *ancien régime* and roots in Caribbean and Native American practice, a suite of pre-Raphaelite paintings by Texas artist Kermit

Oliver, American glassware by Josiah McElheny that acknowledges the informing spirit of both Viennese and Venetian traditions, work by a Japanese-American artist, Gajin Fujita, in a traditional Hispanic idiom, etc.

In the process, two operating strategies presented themselves. First, rather than asking the post-minimalist question, "How rough can it get and still remain meaningful?" I found myself asking the cosmopolitan question: "How smooth can it get and still resist rationalization?" This, because, in a post-industrial world in which everything is presumed to be temporary, nothing need *look* temporary, nor look the same. Second, in order to maintain a substrata of coherence while still privileging exuberance, I found myself selecting works that complemented one another as colors do, pairing works that define a category of practice while sharing no attributes beyond those that define the category. The works of Ken Price and Ellsworth Kelly complement one another in this sense, defining the field of monochrome abstraction without sharing any secondary attributes. The paintings of Bridget Riley and Pia Fries, the spatial treatments of Josiah McElheny and Takashi Murakami, and the wall treatments of Jim Isermann and Gajin Fujita are also complementary in just this sense.

Gradually, the works began arranging themselves in larger constellations of concern. Taken together, the films of Sarah Morris, Stephen Prina, and Kenneth Anger; the photographs of Jeff Burton; and the sculptures of Ken Price and James Lee Byars constitute a short discourse on the erotics of surface. All the films — from Nic Nicosia's narrative of a suburban family performing an episode of *Father Knows Best* to Jane and Louise Wilson's montaged account of a Russian space launch — concern themselves with fantasies of redemption and aspiration. The paintings of Frederick Hammersley, Bridget Riley, Jo Baer, Ellsworth Kelly, and Jesús Rafael Soto, without overlapping, define a field of low-temperature abstraction, which Jim Isermann, Jennifer Steinkamp, and Jorge Pardo exploit beyond the realm of painting; which Jessica Stockholder affectionately deconstructs; and for which Alexis Smith provides a whimsical teleology. Another constellation of works by Jim Isermann, Josiah McElheny, Darryl Montana, Jorge Pardo, Marine Hugonnier, Alexis Smith, and Takashi Murakami test the broad interface of fine art, décor, and design.

Thus, I had no sooner embarked upon the purportedly earnest activity of curating, haphazardly creating networks of visual confluence and cross-reference, than it became clear to me that, by distinguishing my exhibition from the biennial tradition, I was also expanding its traditional mandate. Biennial exhibitions have always been designed to privilege the regional, ethnic, and gender diversity of the artists exhibited. They have been so successful in doing this, in fact, that, at the present moment, one can hardly do otherwise. Such exhibitions, however, have also tended to privilege art made in the dominant postminimal style by mid-career artists of a single generation. In the process of solving my cosmopolitan acrostic, proceeding through the field logic of complements and constellations, I found myself expanding this narrow generational aperture, selecting works by artists spanning a half-century of contemporary art history — revealing, in the process, a host of cross-generational influences and affinities.

Moreover, having opened my field of selection to a multiplicity of cultural influences, I found that radical stylistic diversity was virtually unavoidable. Somehow, it seemed, modernist, post-minimalist, and post-conceptual styles of various flavors and aromas were going to co-exist in the space. They would share that space with Gajin Fujita's wall graffiti and Darryl Montana's Mardi Gras costumes — works whose penchant for cosmopolitan sociability and historical stylistic development mirrors high art practice. Traditionally, international exhibitions that celebrate myths of cultural autonomy have included outsider art whose creators may be considered absolutely autonomous — who, in Peter Schjeldahl's phrase, constitute a "culture of one." By privileging the cosmopolitan, I gained access to an entirely different field of outsider practice, which, since it is no more outside than anything else in the exhibition, fits seamlessly into the ambient chaos.

Amazingly enough, I had the foresight to expect the ambient chaos, simply on account of my catholic tastes. Thus, I decided early on to accommodate S I T E Santa Fe's building to the art rather than asking the artists to accommodate their work to the local site, as is usually done. My first act, in fact, when I was asked about the possibility of curating this exhibition, was to contact Graft Design and solicit their complicity. Our idea from the beginning was to make a space that would make a place for everything— to design a melting pot in which nothing melts. Our general strategy was to invent a space invested with a sense of occasion and rich historical precedents. Ultimately, we created a design that is part Italian palazzo and part informal garden. As a palazzo, the *Beau Monde* building has a processional approach, a façade, an entry hall, a grand hall, and a chapel; it has a mirrored ballroom salon, an elevated petit salon, a grand salon, and three withdrawing rooms. As a garden, it is patterned as a flow-through, peripatetic space with a grand vista that extends from the entrance, diagonally through the building, and out a new window; it has various tantalizing invitations in the form of glimpses and glowing doorways, and an unfolding sequence of visible destinations.

Thus the actual positioning of the works of art had less to do with arranging objects than with choreo-graphing the ideal viewing territories each work demanded. Some of the works in the exhibition, like Jesús Rafael Soto's wall construction, Gajin Fujita's painting, and James Lee Byars' marble sculpture, were designed to be walked by. They were so sited. Some of the works, like Alexis Smith's and Jessica Stockholder's installations, were designed to be walked through, and these were given their transits. Some works, like Josiah McElheny's installation, Jeff Burton's photographs, and Kermit Oliver's paintings, were best to be among. These were given their discrete spaces. Most of the works of art in the exhibition, however, were designed to be approached from a distance, thus a great deal of the planning went into mak-ing them directly approachable; the rest of the design planning went into making the whole space cohesive while complicating this subliminal smoothness by investing each space with its own fictional ambience. For whatever it's worth, we were able to do this to our own satisfaction, and virtually no design work was done on site. A few features were added, a few subtracted, but, basically, we built in Santa Fe what we designed in Los Angeles.

What I had not foreseen was the extent to which shifting the emphasis of the exhibition toward the cosmopolitan and directing its tone toward the high-spirited and lighthearted would influence the "look" of the show. It soon became apparent, however, that the confident accommodation of disparate cultural influences in works of art expresses itself, in practice, as a series of bravura solutions to problems of arrangement and articulation. Exhibitions that aspire to communicate the psychological circumstances of cultural identity, I realized, tend to be composed of art that states problems. The art in *Beau Monde* aspired to solve problems, on the assumption that the visible resolution of cultural dissonance has its moral and intellectual consequences, its social allegories, its uses and functions.

Looking at the work after it was selected and before it was installed, I discovered further that, in works of art, successful cross-cultural engagement (or cultural impurity, if you will) manifests itself in two distinct ways. The confluent cultures either express themselves in the inclusive, intricate complexity of *bricolage* or in the simplicity of abstract structures arising at generalized points of cultural intersection. Cosmopolitan art, I quickly realized, is, almost of necessity, either simpler or more complex than monocultural production. This, I think, accounts for the unusual division of works in the exhibition between abstract simplicity and ebullient complexity—between, for example, the elegant rigor of Ellsworth Kelly's New England "Frenchness" and the gorgeous profusion of Darryl Montana's Caribbean "Frenchness."

The aspect of cosmopolitan art that I probably understood beforehand, but had never successfully articulated, is that, in its radical simplicity and ebullient complexity, it tends to privilege the interpretive instincts of the beholder over any internalized cultural presumptions. This, in turn, tends to privilege the radical sociability of the work in congress and in situ. As a consequence, if you ask me what the assembly and display of all this art in a redesigned space in Santa Fe, New Mexico, might mean, I can only guess. My artist friend, Ed Ruscha, who is represented in this exhibition, once remarked to me that since he and I beheld his finished work at about the same time, we both had an equal shot at guessing what it might mean. This is even more the case with an exhibition, since the curator's job is not to create meaning or to impose meaning on works of art, but to create the circumstances out of which meaning might arise—circumstances that might prove meaningful to the beholder. Finally, all I can offer is my own assurance that the exhibition, at its best, resembles my idea of a "beautiful world." If it is not your idea of a beautiful world, I can only hope that the exhibition articulates options and strategies out of which other beautiful worlds might be created.

September 2001

Las Vegas, Nevada

Kenneth Anger

Born 1930 in Santa Monica, California. Lives and works in Los Angeles, California.

Filmography

Lucifer Rising, 1980
Invocation of My Demon Brother, 1969
Kustom Kar Kommandos, 1965
Scorpio Rising, 1963
Inauguration of the Pleasure Dome, 1954-55
Eaux d'Artifice, 1953
Le Jeune Homme et la Mort, 1951
Rabbit's Moon, 1950
The Love That Whirls, 1949
Puce Moment, 1949
Fireworks, 1947
Drastic Demise, 1945
Escape Episode, 1944
The Nest, 1943
Prisoner of Mars, 1942
Tinsel Tree, 1941
Who Has Been Rocking My Dreamboat, 1941
Ferdinand the Bull, 1937

Selected Solo Exhibitions

2000 *Kenneth Anger Retrospective*
Seattle Art Museum, Washington

1999 *Kenneth Anger's Icons*
Zero One Gallery, Los Angeles, California

1996 *Kenneth Anger's Icons*
Roy G. Biv Gallery, Palm Springs, California

1995 *Kenneth Anger's Icons*
Killer Pix Gallery, Hollywood, California

1993 *Magick Lantern Cycle*
The Andy Warhol Museum,
Pittsburgh, Pennsylvania

Kenneth Anger's Icons
The Andy Warhol Museum,
Pittsburgh, Pennsylvania

1992 *Kenneth Anger's Icons*
Courthouse Gallery, New York, New York

1991 *Kenneth Anger's Icons*
Galerie agnès b., Paris, France

1990 *Kenneth Anger's Icons*
Consulat de France, Vienna, Austria

1985 *Kenneth Anger Retrospective*
Cinémathèque Française, Paris, France

1982 *Magick Lantern Cycle*
Anthology Film Archives, New York, New York

1980 *Kenneth Anger Retrospective*
Whitney Museum of American Art,
New York, New York

Selected Film Festivals

2001 *44th San Francisco International Film Festival*
San Francisco, California

1970 *American Avant-Garde*
Anthology Film Archives, New York, New York

1966 *American Avant-Garde*
The Museum of Modern Art,
New York, New York

1953 *Avant-Garde Americain*
Cinémathèque Française, Paris, France

Kustom Kar Kommandos, 1965
16 mm film, 3 minutes

Jo Baer

Born 1929 in Seattle, Washington. Lives and works in Amsterdam, The Netherlands.

University of Washington, Seattle, Washington
New School for Social Research, New York, New York

Represented by **Galerie Paul Andriesse**, Amsterdam,
The Netherlands

Selected Solo Exhibitions

2001 Stedelijk Museum, Amsterdam, The Netherlands

1993 Paley / Levy Galleries, Moore College of Art
and Design, Philadelphia, Pennsylvania

Rijksmuseum Kröller-Müller,
Otterloo, The Netherlands

1986 *Paintings from the Past Decade 1975-1985*
Stedelijk Van Abbemuseum,
Eindhoven, The Netherlands

1982 Riverside Studios (collaboration with
Bruce Robbins), London, England

1980 112 Workshop (collaboration with
Bruce Robbins), New York, New York

1978 Scottish Arts Council Gallery,
Edinburgh, Scotland

Douglas Hyde Gallery, Trinity College,
Dublin, Ireland

Schilderijen 1962-1975
Stedelijk Van Abbemuseum,
Eindhoven, The Netherlands

1977 *Paintings 1962-1975*
Museum of Modern Art, Oxford, England

1975 Whitney Museum of American Art,
New York, New York

1971 *Paintings from 1962-1963*
School of Visual Arts, New York, New York

Selected Group Exhibitions

2000 *Von Edgar Degas bis Gerhard Richter*
Kunstmuseum Winterthur, Switzerland.
Traveled to National Gallery, Kinsky Palace,
Prague, Czech Republic; Rupertinum,
Museum für moderne und zeitgenössische
Kunst, Salzburg, Austria; Westfälisches
Landesmuseum für Kunst und
Kulturgeschichte, Münster, Germany; and
Neues Museum, Staatliches Museum für
Kunst und Design, Nürnberg, Germany

*Modern and Contemporary Art:
Spotlight on the Collection*
The Museum of Fine Arts, Houston, Texas

1999 *The American Century: Art and Culture
1900-2000* (Part II, 1950-2000)
Whitney Museum of American Art,
New York, New York

1997 *The Pursuit of Painting*
Irish Museum of Modern Art, Dublin, Ireland

1995 *From the Collection: Abstraction,
Pure and Impure*
The Museum of Modern Art,
New York, New York

1994 *From Minimal to Conceptual Art:
Works from the Dorothy and
Herbert Vogel Collection*
National Gallery of Art, Washington, D.C.

1989 *Abstraction, Geometry, Painting:
Selected Geometric Abstract Painting
in America Since 1945*
Albright-Knox Art Gallery, Buffalo, New York.
Traveled to Center for the Fine Arts, Miami,
Florida; Milwaukee Art Museum, Wisconsin;
and Yale University Art Gallery, New Haven,
Connecticut

1988 *La Couleur Seule*
Musée St. Pierre, Lyon, France

1984 *The British Art Show:
Old Allegiances and New Directions*
City of Birmingham Museum and Art Gallery,
and Ikon Gallery, Birmingham, England.
Traveled to Royal Scottish Academy,
Edinburgh, Scotland; Mappin Art Gallery,
Sheffield, England; and Southampton Art
Gallery, England

Ouverture
Castello di Rivoli, Museo d'Arte
Contemporanea, Torino, Italy

1968 *Documenta IV*
Kassel, Germany

1966 *Systemic Painting*
Solomon R. Guggenheim Museum,
New York, New York

page 34   *H. Arcuata*, 1971
Oil on canvas, 22 x 96 x 4 inches

V. Speculum, 1970
Oil on canvas, 80 x 22 x 4 inches

Jeff Burton

Born 1963 in Anaheim, California. Lives and works in Los Angeles, California.

1989 California Institute of the Arts, Valencia, M.F.A.
1985 Texas Christian University, Fort Worth, B.F.A.

Represented by **Casey Kaplan 10-6**, New York, New York; **Sadie Coles HQ**, London, England; and **Taka Ishii Gallery**, Tokyo, Japan

Selected Solo Exhibitions

2001 Casey Kaplan 10-6, New York, New York

Galerie Emmanuel Perrotin, Paris, France

2000 Sadie Coles HQ, London, England

1999 Sadie Coles HQ, London, England

1998 Taka Ishii Gallery, Tokyo, Japan

Casey Kaplan 10-6, New York, New York

Galleri Nicolai Wallner, Copenhagen, Denmark

1996 Casey Kaplan 10-6, New York, New York

1995 Casey Kaplan 10-6, New York, New York

Selected Group Exhibitions

2001 *The Americans. New Art.*
Barbican Gallery, London, England

2000 *Man*
Arken Museum for Moderne Kunst,
Ishoj, Denmark

Garden Party
No Limits Events Gallery, Milan, Italy

1999 *Photography: An Expanded View*
Guggenheim Museum, Bilbao, Spain

Drive-by
South London Gallery, England

Contemporary Photography
Kerlin Gallery, Dublin, Ireland

1998 *The Erotic Sublime (Slave to the Rhythm)*
Galerie Thaddaeus Ropac, Salzburg, Austria

1997 *Stills: Emerging Photography in the 1990s*
Walker Art Center, Minneapolis, Minnesota

Highlights from the Permanent Collection
Museum of Contemporary Art,
North Miami, Florida

1996 *Stream of Consciousness: 8 Los Angeles Artists*
University Art Museum, University of California—
Santa Barbara

page 55 *Untitled #149 (upholstery tacks)*, 2001
Cibachrome print, 40 x 60 inches

pages 86-87 *Untitled #156 (Fragonard)*, 2001
Cibachrome print, 40 x 60 inches

page 52 *Untitled #126 (live to ride)*, 2000
Cibachrome print, 40 x 60 inches

page 47 *Untitled #137 (globe)*, 2000
Cibachrome print, 40 x 60 inches

page 54 *Untitled #48 (afghan)*, 1997
Cibachrome print, 60 x 40 inches

James Lee Byars

Born 1932 in Detroit, Michigan. Died 1997 in Cairo, Egypt.

Wayne State University, Detroit, Michigan
Merill-Palmer Institute, Detroit, Michigan

The James Lee Byars Estate is represented by
Michael Werner Gallery, New York, New York,
and Cologne, Germany

Selected Solo Exhibitions

1999   *The Epitaph of Con. Art is which Questions
have disappeared?*
Kestner Gesellschaft, Hannover, Germany

1998   The Arts Club of Chicago, Illinois

1997   *James Lee Byars: The Palace of Perfect*
Fundação de Serralves, Porto, Portugal

1996   *The Monument To Language*
The Henry Moore Institute, Leeds, England

1995   *James Lee Byars: Perfect is my death word*
Neues Museum Weserburg, Bremen, Germany

1994   *James Lee Byars: The Perfect Moment*
Institut Valencia d'Art Modern,
Centre del Carme, Valencia, Spain

1989   *James Lee Byars: The Palace of Good Luck*
Castello di Rivoli, Museo d'Arte
Contemporanea, Torino, Italy

1986   *James Lee Byars: The Philosophical Palace*
Kunsthalle Düsseldorf, Germany

1983   Stedelijk Van Abbemuseum, Eindhoven,
The Netherlands

1977   Wide White Space Gallery, Antwerp, Belgium

1964   *1 x 50 Foot Drawing*
Carnegie Institute, Pittsburgh, Pennsylvania

Selected Group Exhibitions

1996   *Drawings: Acquisitions 1992-1996*
Musée national d'art Moderne,
Centre Georges Pompidou, Paris, France

1988   *Couplet 2*
Stedelijk Museum, Amsterdam,
The Netherlands

1987   *Documenta VIII*
Kassel, Germany

1986   *Choices: Making an Art of Everyday Life*
New Museum of Contemporary Art,
New York, New York

Venice Biennale
Italy

1984   *Twentieth Century Sculpture*
Merienpark, Basel, Switzerland

1983   *New Art at the Tate Gallery*
The Tate Gallery, London, England

1982   *Documenta VII*
Kassel, Germany

1980   *Venice Biennale*
Italy

1977   *Documenta VI*
Kassel, Germany

1976   *Drawing Now*
The Museum of Modern Art,
New York, New York

pages 22-23   *Eros*, 1992
White Thassos marble (2 parts),
26¾ x 67 x 13½ inches overall

Pia Fries

Born 1955 in Beromünster, Switzerland. Lives and works in Düsseldorf, Germany.

1980-86 Kunstakademie Düsseldorf, Germany

1977-80 Hochschule für Gestaltung und Kunst, Lucerne, Switzerland

Represented by **Mai 36 Galerie**, Zürich, Switzerland; **Galerie Rolf Ricke**, Cologne, Germany; **CRG Gallery**, New York, New York; **Christopher Grimes Gallery**, Los Angeles, California; **Philip Nelson Gallery**, Paris, France; **Rodolphe Janssen**, Brussels, Belgium; and **The Box**, Torino, Italy

Selected Solo Exhibitions

2001 Museum Moderne Kunst, Otterndorf, Germany

2000 Galerie Rolf Ricke, Cologne, Germany

Overbeck-Gesellschaft, Lübeck, Germany

1999 *Parsen und Module*
Kunsthalle Göppingen, Germany

Galerie Nelson, Paris, France

1997 Aargauer Kunsthaus, Aarau, Switzerland

Kunstverein Freiburg, Freiburg im Breisgau, Germany

1994 Mai 36 Galerie, Zürich, Switzerland

1992 Bonner Kunstverein, Bonn, Germany

Kunstmuseum Lucerne, Switzerland

1988 Galerie Rüdiger Schöttle, Munich, Germany

1987 Museum Kurhaus Kleve, Germany

Selected Group Exhibitions

2001 *L.A. International*
Christopher Grimes Gallery, Los Angeles

Surface and Paint
CRG Gallery, New York, New York

2000 *Von Edgar Degas bis Gerhard Richter*
Kunstmuseum Winterthur, Switzerland.
Traveled to National Gallery, Kinsky Palace, Prague, Czech Republic; Rupertinum, Museum für moderne und zeitgenössische Kunst, Salzburg, Austria; Westfälisches Landesmuseum für Kunst und Kulturgeschichte, Münster, Germany; and Neues Museum, Staatliches Museum für Kunst und Design, Nürnberg, Germany

2356 KM
Neue Manege Moskau, Moscow, Russia

1999 *Super-Abstraction*
The Box, Torino, Italy

Venice Biennale
Italy

Special Offer
Kasseler Kunstverein, Kassel, Germany

1996 *En Heluetes Förvandung*
Kulturhuset, Stockholm, Sweden

Nähe und Ferne
Stadtmuseum, Sofia, Bulgaria

1990 *Szene Schweiz*
Mannheimer Kunstverein, Mannheim, Germany

1986 *Freibhaus 4*
Kunstmuseum Düsseldorf, Germany

1984 *Sammlung Klinker*
Kunstmuseum Bochum, Germany

page 26 *quinto*, 1994-95
Oil on wood (5 panels),
78¾ x 239⅛ inches overall

Gajin Fujita

Born 1972 in Los Angeles, California. Lives and works in Los Angeles, California.

2000 University of Nevada, Las Vegas, M.F.A.
1997 Otis College of Art and Design,
Westchester, California, B.F.A.

Represented by **Kravets/Wehby Gallery**, New York,
New York; **Galerie Rolf Ricke**, Cologne, Germany; and
L.A. Louver Gallery, Venice, California

Selected Solo Exhibitions

2002 L.A. Louver Gallery, Venice, California

2001 Galerie Rolf Ricke, Cologne, Germany

2000 Kravets/Wehby Gallery, New York, New York

Thesis Show
Donna Beam Fine Art Gallery,
University of Nevada, Las Vegas

Selected Group Exhibitions

2001 *Hard-Boiled Wonderland*
Luckman Gallery, California State University,
Los Angeles

Rogue Wave: 11 Artists from Los Angeles
L.A. Louver Gallery, Venice, California

The Dreams Stuff is Made Of
Art Frankfurt, Germany

Casino 2001
Stedelijk Museum voor Actuele Kunst,
Gent, Belgium

New American Talent: The Fifteenth Exhibition
Texas Fine Arts Association, Austin.
Traveled in Texas to Texarkana Regional Arts
and Humanities Council; Firehouse Gallery,
Del Rio Council for the Arts; Blue Star Art

Space, San Antonio; and Buddy Holly Center,
Lubbock

2000 *Radar Love*
Gallery Marabini, Bologna, Italy

Other Paintings
Huntington Beach Art Center, California

pages 32-33   *South Cali*, 2001
Acrylic, spray paint, gold and silver leaf
on wood panel (12 panels),
48 x 192 x 2½ inches overall

page 10   With Alex Kizu (K2SCrew)
and Jessie Simon (KGB Crew)
Graffiti Beau Monde, 2001
Spray paint, 24 x 100 feet

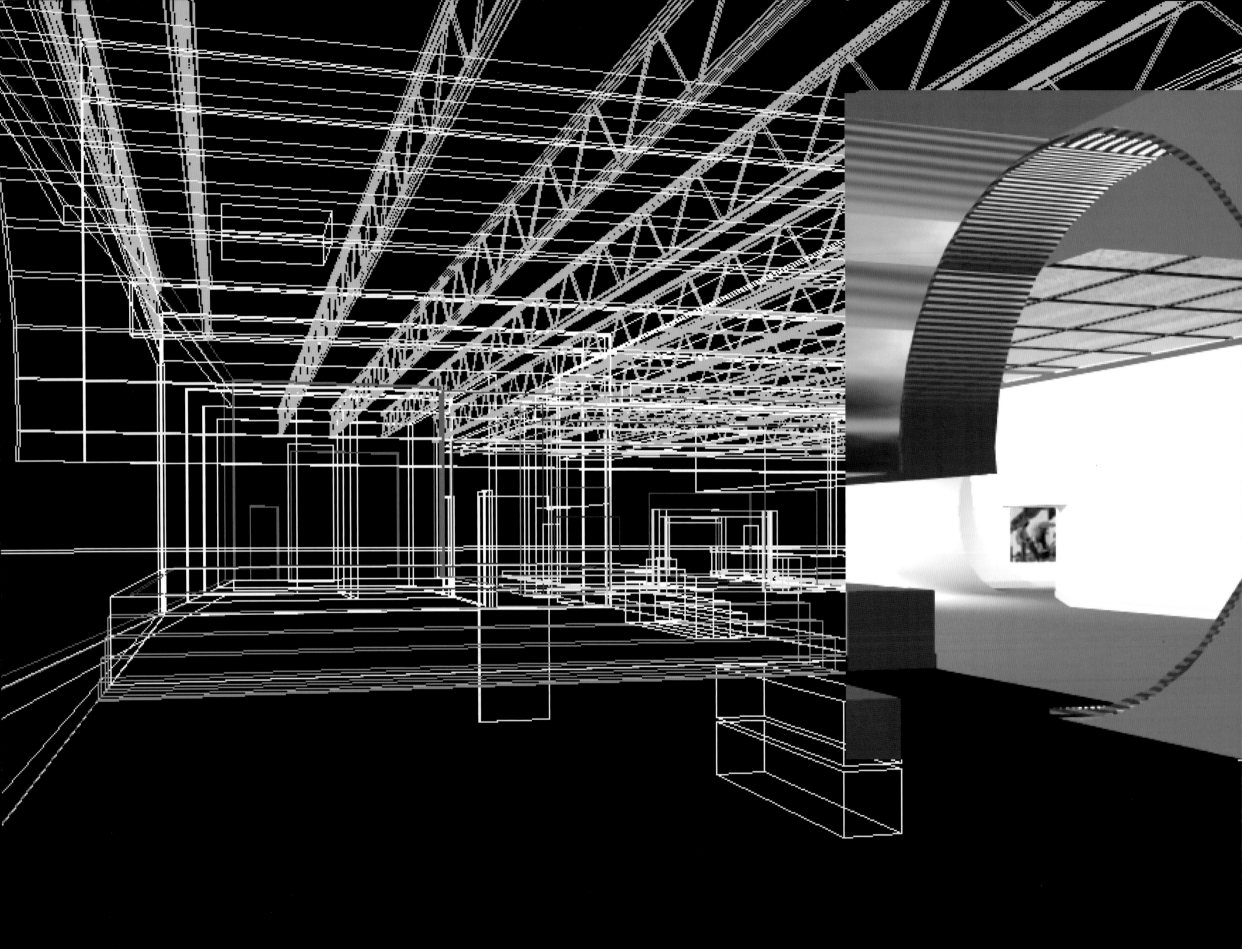

Graft Design

Founded in 1998. Offices in Los Angeles, California, and Berlin, Germany.

Gregor Hoheisel
born 1967 in Hamburg, Germany

1996 Technische Universität Braunschweig,
Germany, Dipl. Ing. Arch.

1988 Fachhochschule Hamburg, Germany

Christoph Korner
born 1969 in Münich, Germany

1999 University of California,
Los Angeles, M. Arch.

1995 Technische Universität Braunschweig,
Germany, Dipl. Ing. Arch.

1993 Southern Californian
Institute of Architecture,
Los Angeles

1992 Technische Universität Braunschweig,
Germany

Lars Krückeberg
born 1967 in Hannover, Germany

1998 Southern Californian
Institute of Architecture,
Los Angeles, M. Arch.

1996 Technische Universität Braunschweig,
Germany, Dipl. Ing. Arch.

1993 Universitá degli Studi di Firenze,
Florence, Italy

1992 Technische Universität Braunschweig,
Germany

Wolfram Putz
born 1968 in Kiel, Germany

1998 Southern Californian
Institute of Architecture,
Los Angeles, M. Arch.

1995 Technische Universität Braunschweig,
Germany, Dipl. Ing. Arch.

1993 University of Utah,
Salt Lake City

1992 Technische Universität Braunschweig,
Germany

Thomas Willemeit
born 1967 in Remscheid, Germany

1998 Technische Universität Braunschweig,
Germany, Dipl. Ing. Arch.

Selected Projects and Commissions

2001 *4 Sights*, art and architecture exhibition and
workshop, Riga, Latvia

Seeing, exhibition design for the Los Angeles
County Museum of Art, California

Zeal Pictures, interior design for a hybrid city
block at the Spree, Berlin, Germany

Wine Country Grill, interior design
of restaurant in Los Angeles, California

2000 *Surveillance,* installation project
(with the artist group MADE),
New York, New York

Neue Sentimentale, interior design for
a production company (with JP Flack),
Marina del Rey, California

Earthlink, design concepts for
Earthlink headquarters (with Wirt Design),
Pasadena, California

Salve, media landscape for Goethe Institut,
Los Angeles, California

1999 *Will2K*, music video set design
for Will Smith (with JP Flack),
Los Angeles, California

Lenne Preis, design competition for central
plaza (1st prize), Berlin, Germany

AMMO, interior design of restaurant in
Los Angeles, California

Brad Pitt residence, interior design of
guesthouse and studio (with Kevin Haley),
Hollywood, California

pages 1, 94-95   With Dave Hickey, exhibition
design for *Beau Monde: Toward a Redeemed
Cosmopolitanism*

page 15   *Kissy Kissy Touchy Touchy*, 2001
Artificial flora, lava rocks, audio,
dimensions variable

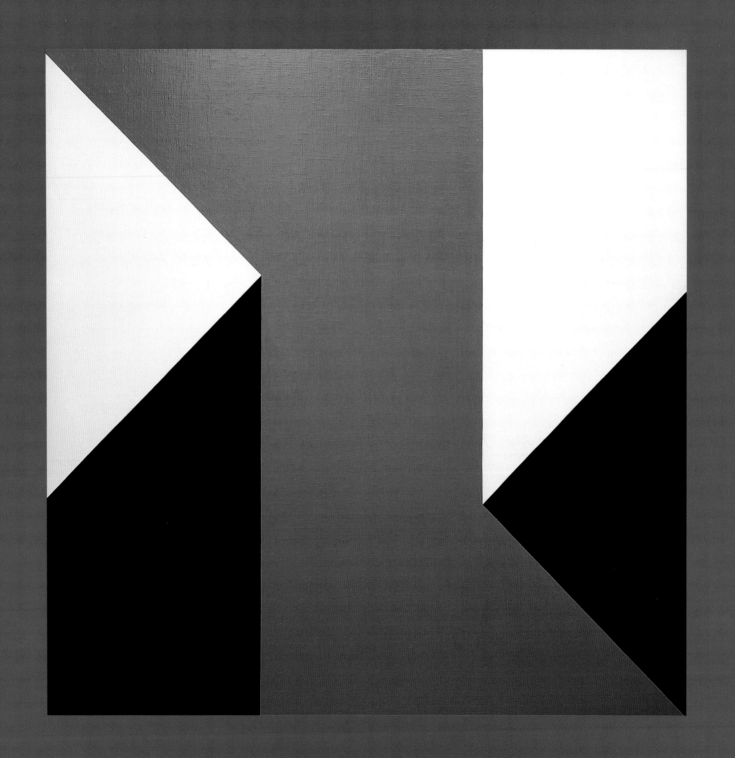

Frederick Hammersley

Born 1919 in Salt Lake City, Utah. Lives and works in Albuquerque, New Mexico.

1950 Jepson Art School, Los Angeles, California
1947 Chouinard Art School, Los Angeles, California
1945 École des Beaux-Arts, Paris, France
1942 Chouinard Art School, Los Angeles, California
1938 University of Idaho, Southern Branch, Pocatello

Represented by **L.A. Louver Gallery**, Venice, California; **Richard Levy Gallery**, Albuquerque, New Mexico; and **Gary Snyder Fine Art**, New York, New York

Selected Solo Exhibitions

1999- *Visual Puns and Hard-Edge Poems*
2000 Laguna Art Museum, Laguna Beach, California. Traveled to University of New Mexico, Albuquerque, and Museum of Fine Arts, Santa Fe, New Mexico

1999 *I've Been Here All the While*
   L.A. Louver Gallery, Venice, California

1995 *Hard-Edge & Organic Paintings 1947-1991*
   Modernism, San Francisco, California

1993 Mulvane Art Museum of Washburn University, Topeka, Kansas

1989- *Paris, Berlin, Albuquerque*
1990 California State University, Northridge

1984 *Poles a Part*
   Hoshour Gallery, Albuquerque, New Mexico

1981 *Rules and Exceptions*
   L.A. Louver Gallery, Venice, California

1975 *A Retrospective Exhibition*
   Art Museum, University of New Mexico, Albuquerque

1969 Art Museum, University of New Mexico, Albuquerque

1965 Santa Barbara Museum of Art, California

1962- *Frederick Hammersley*
1963 California Palace of the Legion of Honor, San Francisco. Traveled to Art Center in La Jolla, California

1961 Pasadena Art Museum, California

Selected Group Exhibitions

1994- *Still Working*
1996 Corcoran Gallery of Art, Washington, D.C. Traveled to Chicago Cultural Center, Illinois; New School for Social Research, New York, New York; Virginia Beach Center for the Arts, Virginia; University of Southern California, Fisher Gallery, Los Angeles; and Portland Museum of Art, Oregon

1979- *The First Western States Biennial Exhibition*
1980 Denver Art Museum, Colorado. Traveled to National Collection of Fine Arts, Washington, D.C.; San Francisco Museum of Modern Art, California; and Seattle Art Museum, Washington.

1979- *Here & Now: 35 Artists in New Mexico*
1980 The Albuquerque Museum, New Mexico

1977 *35th Biennial*
   Corcoran Gallery of Art, Washington, D.C.

California: 5 Footnotes to Modern Art History
   Los Angeles County Museum of Art, California

Private Images: Photographs by Painters
Los Angeles County Museum of Art, California

1974 *Geometric Abstraction*
   University of Nebraska, Lincoln and Omaha, and Hastings College, Nebraska

1969- *Computer Drawings*
1970 Institute of Contemporary Art, London, England. Traveled to Simon Fraser University, Burnaby, Canada

1965 *The Responsive Eye*
   The Museum of Modern Art, New York, New York

1962 *Geometric Abstraction in America*
   Whitney Museum of American Art, New York, New York

1959- *Purist Painting*
1960 American Federation of Arts

1959- *Four Abstract Classicists: Benjamin, Feitelson,*
1960 *Hammersley, McLaughlin*
   San Francisco Museum of Modern Art, California. Traveled to Los Angeles County Museum of Art, California; Institute of Contemporary Art, London, England; and Queen's University, Belfast, Ireland

page 96 *Side Saddle*, 1979
Oil on canvas, 45 x 45 inches

page 25 *Love Me, Love My Dog*, 1972
Oil on canvas, 45 x 45 inches

Marine Hugonnier

Born 1969 in Paris, France. Lives and works in London, England.

2001 Brighton Film School, England
1999 The Delfina Studio Trust, London, England
1999 Le Fresnoy Studio National des Arts Contemporains, Lille, France

Represented by **Galerie Chantal Crousel**, Paris, France

Selected Solo Exhibitions

2001 Annet Gelink Gallery, Amsterdam, The Netherlands

Kerstin Engholm Galerie, Vienna, Austria

Max Wigram Gallery, London, England

Centro Galego de Arte Contemporánea, Santiago de Compostela, Spain

2000 Galerie Chantal Crousel, Paris, France

fig-1, London, England

Art Unlimited
Art 32 Basel, Switzerland

Selected Group Exhibitions

2001 *Traversées*
Musée d'art Moderne de la ville de Paris, France

Unreal time video
The Korean Culture and Arts Foundation, Seoul, South Korea

Squatters
Fundação de Serralves, Porto, Portugal

Movimientos Inmoviles
Museo de Arte Moderno, Buenos Aires, Argentina

2000 *Mexico City Cinema Festival*
Cinemax World Trade Center, Mexico City, Mexico

Vivre sa vie
Tramway, Glasgow, Scotland

1997 Project for *TV Mobile*
Le Consortium, Centre d'art Contemporain, Dijon, France

1996 *Subjective Play*
Spot, New York, New York

1995 *Au-delà des apparences*
Galerie des Archives, Paris, France

1994 Fuel Gallery, Seattle, Washington

page 49 *Flower*, 2000
Seasonal flowers, spray paint for fresh flowers, vase, dimensions variable

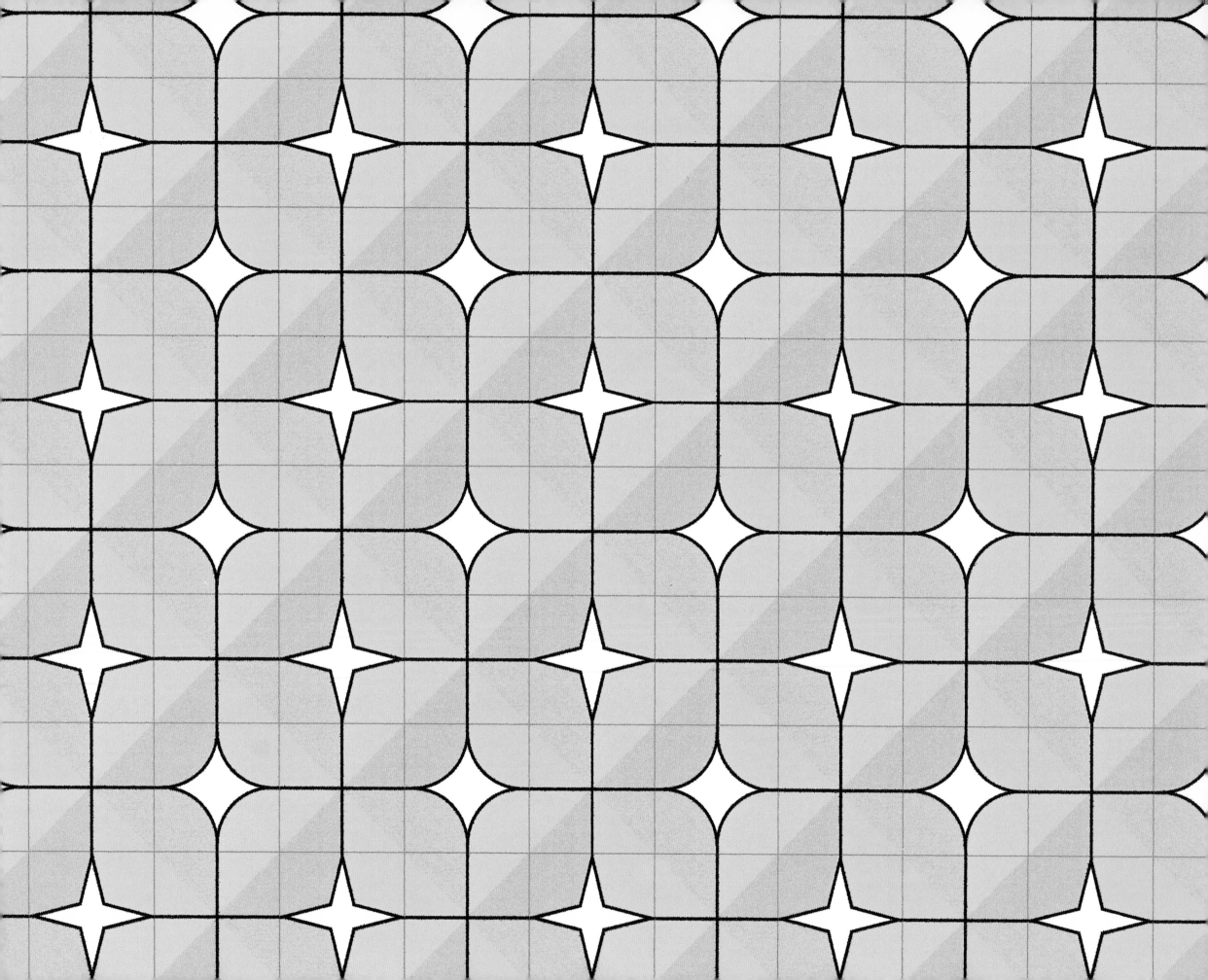

Jim Isermann

Born 1955 in Kenosha, Wisconsin. Lives and works in Palm Springs, California.

1980 **California Institute of the Arts,** Valencia, M.F.A.
1977 **University of Wisconsin,** Milwaukee, B.F.A.

Represented by **Corvi-Mora,** London, England;
Feature Inc., New York, New York; and **Richard Telles
Fine Art,** Los Angeles, California

Selected Solo Exhibitions

2002 Corvi-Mora, London, England

2001 Richard Telles Fine Art, Los Angeles, California

 Feature Inc., New York, New York

2000 Portikus, Frankfurt, Germany

 Galerie Praz-Delavallade, Paris, France

1999 *Vega*
 Le Magasin, Centre National d'art
 Contemporain de Grenoble, France

 Camden Art Centre, London, England

1998 *Fifteen: Jim Isermann Survey*
 The Institute of Visual Arts, University
 of Wisconsin—Milwaukee. Traveled to
 DiverseWorks, Houston, Texas;
 The University of North Texas Art Gallery,
 Denton; The Santa Monica Museum of Art,
 California; The Weatherspoon Art Gallery,
 University of North Carolina—Greensboro;
 and Institute of Contemporary Art,
 University of Pennsylvania—Philadelphia

1997 Ynglingagatan 1, Stockholm, Sweden

 Studio Guenzani, Milan, Italy

Selected Group Exhibitions

2001 *Patterns: Between Object and Arabesque*
 Kunsthallen Brandts Klædefabrik,
 Odense, Denmark

2000 *Jim Isermann: Logic Rules*
 The RISD Museum, Providence, Rhode Island

 Made in California: NOW
 Los Angeles County Museum of Art,
 LACMALab, California

 *What if: Art on the Verge
 of Architecture and Design*
 Moderna Museet, Stockholm, Sweden

 *Ultralounge: The Return of Social Space
 (with Cocktails)*
 DiverseWorks, Houston, Texas. Traveled to
 University of South Florida Contemporary Art
 Museum, Tampa

1999 *In the Midst of Things*
 Bournville, Birmingham, England

1998 *Homemade Champagne*
 Claremont Graduate University, California

1997 *Sunshine & Noir: Art in Los Angeles,
 1960-1997*
 Louisiana Museum of Modern Art,
 Humlebaek, Denmark. Traveled to Castello di
 Rivoli, Museo d'Arte Contemporanea, Torino,
 Italy; Hayward Gallery, London, England; Haus
 der Kunst, München, Germany; and The UCLA
 Hammer Museum, Los Angeles, California

 Lovecraft
 Centre for Contemporary Art, Glasgow,
 Scotland. Traveled to South London Gallery,
 London, England

1993 *Project Unité*
 Unité d'Habitation, Firminy, France

cover, pages 8-9 *Untitled (0101) (silver),*
2001. Painted vacuum formed ABS plastic
(750 panels), 24 x 24 x 3 inches each
Façade dimensions: 24 x 113 x 5½ feet

Ellsworth Kelly

Born 1923 in Newburgh, New York. Lives and works in Spencertown, New York.

Represented by **Matthew Marks Gallery**, New York, New York

Selected Solo Exhibitions

2001 *Ellsworth Kelly: Blue*
White Cube, London, England

Ellsworth Kelly Relief Paintings 1954-2001
Matthew Marks Gallery, New York, New York

2000 *Ellsworth Kelly at Gemini – New Lithographs*
Gemini G.E.L., Los Angeles, California

1999 *Ellsworth Kelly: Spectrums, 1953-1972*
Mitchell-Innes and Nash Gallery, New York, New York

Ellsworth Kelly: Sculpture for a Large Wall and Other Recent Acquisitions
The Museum of Modern Art, New York, New York

Ellsworth Kelly: The Early Drawings, 1948-1955
Fogg Art Museum, Harvard University, Cambridge, Massachusetts. Traveled to High Museum of Art, Atlanta, Georgia; The Art Institute of Chicago, Illinois; Kunstmuseum Winterthur, Switzerland; Städtische Galerie im Lenbachhaus, Münich, Germany; and Kunstmuseum Bonn, Germany

1998 *Ellsworth Kelly on the Roof*
The Iris and B. Gerald Cantor Roof Garden, The Metropolitan Museum of Art, New York, New York

1996 *Ellsworth Kelly – A Retrospective*
Solomon R. Guggenheim Museum, New York, New York. Traveled to The Museum of Contemporary Art, Los Angeles, California;

Tate Gallery, London, England; and Haus der Kunst, Münich, Germany

1994 *Ellsworth Kelly: The Process of Seeing*
Walker Art Center, Minneapolis, Minnesota

Spencertown: Recent Paintings by Ellsworth Kelly
Anthony d'Offay Gallery, London, England

1992 *Ellsworth Kelly: Les Années Français, 1948-1954*
Galerie Nationale du Jeu de Paume, Paris, France. Traveled to Westfälisches Landesmuseum, Münster, Germany, and National Gallery of Art, Washington, D.C.

Selected Group Exhibitions

2001 *Ornament and Abstraction: The dialogue between non-Western, modern and contemporary art*
Fondation Beyeler, Basel, Switzerland

Tate Modern: Collection 2001
Tate Modern, London, England

2000 *L'inauguration des sculptures de Roy Lichtenstein, Ellsworth Kelly, et Daniel Dezeuze au Jardin des Tuileries*
Le Jardin des Tuileries, Paris, France

Century of Innocence – The History of the White Monochrome
Rooseum Center for Contemporary Art, Malmö, Sweden. Traveled to Liljevalchs Kunsthall, Stockholm, Sweden

Master Drawings from the Cleveland Museum of Art

Cleveland Museum of Art, Ohio. Traveled to The Pierpont Morgan Library, New York, New York

1999 *The American Century: Art and Culture 1900-2000* (Part II, 1950-2000)
Whitney Museum of American Art, New York, New York

1998 *Selections from the Anderson Graphic Arts Collection: Contemporary Portraits*
Fine Arts Museums of San Francisco, California

1997 *20th Anniversaire du Centre National d'Art et de Culture*
Centre Georges Pompidou, Paris, France

1996 *Continuity and Contradiction: A New Look at the Permanent Collection*
Museum of Contemporary Art, San Diego, California

Abstraction in the Twentieth Century: Total Risk, Freedom, Discipline
Solomon R. Guggenheim Museum, New York, New York

1995 *Views from Abroad: European Perspectives on American Art I*
Whitney Museum of American Art, New York, New York. Traveled to Stedelijk Museum, Amsterdam, The Netherlands

Made in America: Ten Centuries of American Art
The Minneapolis Institute of Arts, Minnesota. Traveled to The Saint Louis Art Museum, Missouri; Toledo Museum of Art, Ohio; The Nelson-Atkins Museum of Art, Kansas City, Missouri; and Carnegie Museum of Art, Pittsburgh, Pennsylvania

pages 42-43 *Blue Black Red Green*, 2000
Oil on canvas (4 separate panels),
100 x 484 ½ inches overall

Frederick Hammersley

Born 1919 in Salt Lake City, Utah. Lives and works in Albuquerque, New Mexico.

1950 Jepson Art School, Los Angeles, California
1947 Chouinard Art School, Los Angeles, California
1945 École des Beaux-Arts, Paris, France
1942 Chouinard Art School, Los Angeles, California
1938 University of Idaho, Southern Branch, Pocatello

Represented by **L.A. Louver Gallery**, Venice, California;
Richard Levy Gallery, Albuquerque, New Mexico; and
Gary Snyder Fine Art, New York, New York

Selected Solo Exhibitions

1999- *Visual Puns and Hard-Edge Poems*
2000 Laguna Art Museum, Laguna Beach, California.
Traveled to University of New Mexico,
Albuquerque, and Museum of Fine Arts,
Santa Fe, New Mexico

1999 *I've Been Here All the While*
L.A. Louver Gallery, Venice, California

1995 *Hard-Edge & Organic Paintings 1947-1991*
Modernism, San Francisco, California

1993 Mulvane Art Museum of Washburn University,
Topeka, Kansas

1989- *Paris, Berlin, Albuquerque*
1990 California State University, Northridge

1984 *Poles a Part*
Hoshour Gallery, Albuquerque, New Mexico

1981 *Rules and Exceptions*
L.A. Louver Gallery, Venice, California

1975 *A Retrospective Exhibition*
Art Museum, University of New Mexico,
Albuquerque

1969 Art Museum, University of New Mexico,
Albuquerque

1965 Santa Barbara Museum of Art, California

1962- *Frederick Hammersley*
1963 California Palace of the Legion of Honor,
San Francisco. Traveled to Art Center in
La Jolla, California

1961 Pasadena Art Museum, California

Selected Group Exhibitions

1994- *Still Working*
1996 Corcoran Gallery of Art, Washington, D.C.
Traveled to Chicago Cultural Center, Illinois;
New School for Social Research, New York,
New York; Virginia Beach Center for the Arts,
Virginia; University of Southern California,
Fisher Gallery, Los Angeles; and Portland
Museum of Art, Oregon

1979- *The First Western States Biennial Exhibition*
1980 Denver Art Museum, Colorado. Traveled to
National Collection of Fine Arts, Washington,
D.C.; San Francisco Museum of Modern Art,
California; and Seattle Art Museum,
Washington.

1979- *Here & Now: 35 Artists in New Mexico*
1980 The Albuquerque Museum, New Mexico

1977 *35th Biennial*
Corcoran Gallery of Art, Washington, D.C.

California: 5 Footnotes to Modern Art History
Los Angeles County Museum of Art, California

Private Images: Photographs by Painters
Los Angeles County Museum of Art, California

1974 *Geometric Abstraction*
University of Nebraska, Lincoln and Omaha,
and Hastings College, Nebraska

1969- *Computer Drawings*
1970 Institute of Contemporary Art, London,
England. Traveled to Simon Fraser University,
Burnaby, Canada

1965 *The Responsive Eye*
The Museum of Modern Art, New York,
New York

1962 *Geometric Abstraction in America*
Whitney Museum of American Art,
New York, New York

1959- *Purist Painting*
1960 American Federation of Arts

1959- *Four Abstract Classicists: Benjamin, Feitelson,*
1960 *Hammersley, McLaughlin*
San Francisco Museum of Modern Art,
California. Traveled to Los Angeles County
Museum of Art, California; Institute of
Contemporary Art, London, England; and
Queen's University, Belfast, Ireland

page 96   *Side Saddle*, 1979
Oil on canvas, 45 x 45 inches

page 25   *Love Me, Love My Dog*, 1972
Oil on canvas, 45 x 45 inches

Marine Hugonnier

Born 1969 in Paris, France. Lives and works in London, England.

2001 Brighton Film School, England
1999 The Delfina Studio Trust, London, England
1999 Le Fresnoy Studio National des Arts
Contemporains, Lille, France

Represented by **Galerie Chantal Crousel**, Paris, France

Selected Solo Exhibitions

2001 Annet Gelink Gallery, Amsterdam,
The Netherlands

Kerstin Engholm Galerie, Vienna, Austria

Max Wigram Gallery, London, England

Centro Galego de Arte Contemporánea,
Santiago de Compostela, Spain

2000 Galerie Chantal Crousel, Paris, France

fig-1, London, England

Art Unlimited
Art 32 Basel, Switzerland

Selected Group Exhibitions

2001 *Traversées*
Musée d'art Moderne de la ville de Paris, France

Unreal time video
The Korean Culture and Arts Foundation,
Seoul, South Korea

Squatters
Fundação de Serralves, Porto, Portugal

Movimientos Inmoviles
Museo de Arte Moderno,
Buenos Aires, Argentina

2000 *Mexico City Cinema Festival*
Cinemax World Trade Center,
Mexico City, Mexico

Vivre sa vie
Tramway, Glasgow, Scotland

1997 Project for *TV Mobile*
Le Consortium, Centre d'art Contemporain,
Dijon, France

1996 *Subjective Play*
Spot, New York, New York

1995 *Au-delà des apparences*
Galerie des Archives, Paris, France

1994 Fuel Gallery, Seattle, Washington

page 49 *Flower*, 2000
Seasonal flowers, spray paint for fresh flowers,
vase, dimensions variable

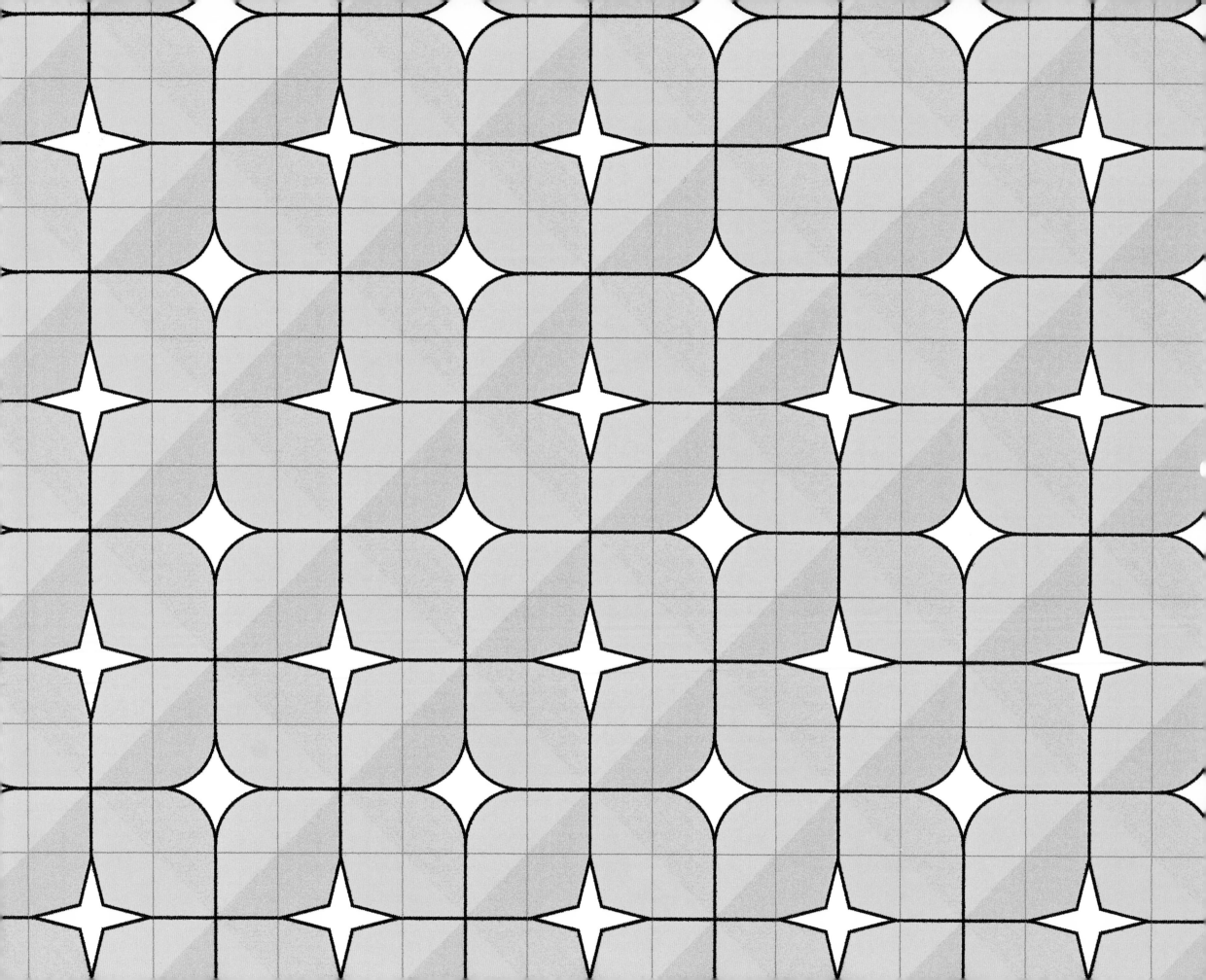

Jim Isermann

Born 1955 in Kenosha, Wisconsin. Lives and works in Palm Springs, California.

1980 **California Institute of the Arts,** Valencia, M.F.A.
1977 **University of Wisconsin,** Milwaukee, B.F.A.

Represented by **Corvi-Mora,** London, England;
Feature Inc., New York, New York; and **Richard Telles
Fine Art,** Los Angeles, California

Selected Solo Exhibitions

2002 Corvi-Mora, London, England

2001 Richard Telles Fine Art, Los Angeles, California

Feature Inc., New York, New York

2000 Portikus, Frankfurt, Germany

Galerie Praz-Delavallade, Paris, France

1999 *Vega*
Le Magasin, Centre National d'art
Contemporain de Grenoble, France

Camden Art Centre, London, England

1998 *Fifteen: Jim Isermann Survey*
The Institute of Visual Arts, University
of Wisconsin—Milwaukee. Traveled to
DiverseWorks, Houston, Texas;
The University of North Texas Art Gallery,
Denton; The Santa Monica Museum of Art,
California; The Weatherspoon Art Gallery,
University of North Carolina—Greensboro;
and Institute of Contemporary Art,
University of Pennsylvania—Philadelphia

1997 Ynglingagatan 1, Stockholm, Sweden

Studio Guenzani, Milan, Italy

Selected Group Exhibitions

2001 *Patterns: Between Object and Arabesque*
Kunsthallen Brandts Klædefabrik,
Odense, Denmark

2000 *Jim Isermann: Logic Rules*
The RISD Museum, Providence, Rhode Island

Made in California: NOW
Los Angeles County Museum of Art,
LACMALab, California

*What if: Art on the Verge
of Architecture and Design*
Moderna Museet, Stockholm, Sweden

*Ultralounge: The Return of Social Space
(with Cocktails)*
DiverseWorks, Houston, Texas. Traveled to
University of South Florida Contemporary Art
Museum, Tampa

1999 *In the Midst of Things*
Bournville, Birmingham, England

1998 *Homemade Champagne*
Claremont Graduate University, California

1997 *Sunshine & Noir: Art in Los Angeles,
1960-1997*
Louisiana Museum of Modern Art,
Humlebaek, Denmark. Traveled to Castello di
Rivoli, Museo d'Arte Contemporanea, Torino,
Italy; Hayward Gallery, London, England; Haus
der Kunst, Münich, Germany; and The UCLA
Hammer Museum, Los Angeles, California

Lovecraft
Centre for Contemporary Art, Glasgow,
Scotland. Traveled to South London Gallery,
London, England

1993 *Project Unité*
Unité d'Habitation, Firminy, France

cover, pages 8-9 *Untitled (0101) (silver),*
2001. Painted vacuum formed ABS plastic
(750 panels), 24 x 24 x 3 inches each
Façade dimensions: 24 x 113 x 5½ feet

Ellsworth Kelly

Born 1923 in Newburgh, New York. Lives and works in Spencertown, New York.

Represented by **Matthew Marks Gallery,** New York, New York

Selected Solo Exhibitions

2001 *Ellsworth Kelly: Blue*
White Cube, London, England

Ellsworth Kelly Relief Paintings 1954-2001
Matthew Marks Gallery, New York, New York

2000 *Ellsworth Kelly at Gemini – New Lithographs*
Gemini G.E.L., Los Angeles, California

1999 *Ellsworth Kelly: Spectrums, 1953-1972*
Mitchell-Innes and Nash Gallery, New York, New York

Ellsworth Kelly: Sculpture for a Large Wall and Other Recent Acquisitions
The Museum of Modern Art, New York, New York

Ellsworth Kelly: The Early Drawings, 1948-1955
Fogg Art Museum, Harvard University, Cambridge, Massachusetts. Traveled to High Museum of Art, Atlanta, Georgia; The Art Institute of Chicago, Illinois; Kunstmuseum Winterthur, Switzerland; Städtische Galerie im Lenbachhaus, Münich, Germany; and Kunstmuseum Bonn, Germany

1998 *Ellsworth Kelly on the Roof*
The Iris and B. Gerald Cantor Roof Garden, The Metropolitan Museum of Art, New York, New York

1996 *Ellsworth Kelly – A Retrospective*
Solomon R. Guggenheim Museum, New York, New York. Traveled to The Museum of Contemporary Art, Los Angeles, California;

Tate Gallery, London, England; and Haus der Kunst, Münich, Germany

1994 *Ellsworth Kelly: The Process of Seeing*
Walker Art Center, Minneapolis, Minnesota

Spencertown: Recent Paintings by Ellsworth Kelly
Anthony d'Offay Gallery, London, England

1992 *Ellsworth Kelly: Les Années Français, 1948-1954*
Galerie Nationale du Jeu de Paume, Paris, France. Traveled to Westfälisches Landesmuseum, Münster, Germany, and National Gallery of Art, Washington, D.C.

Selected Group Exhibitions

2001 *Ornament and Abstraction: The dialogue between non-Western, modern and contemporary art*
Fondation Beyeler, Basel, Switzerland

Tate Modern: Collection 2001
Tate Modern, London, England

2000 *L'inauguration des sculptures de Roy Lichtenstein, Ellsworth Kelly, et Daniel Dezeuze au Jardin des Tuileries*
Le Jardin des Tuileries, Paris, France

Century of Innocence – The History of the White Monochrome
Rooseum Center for Contemporary Art, Malmö, Sweden. Traveled to Liljevalchs Kunsthall, Stockholm, Sweden

Master Drawings from the Cleveland Museum of Art

Cleveland Museum of Art, Ohio. Traveled to The Pierpont Morgan Library, New York, New York

1999 *The American Century: Art and Culture 1900-2000* (Part II, 1950-2000)
Whitney Museum of American Art, New York, New York

1998 *Selections from the Anderson Graphic Arts Collection: Contemporary Portraits*
Fine Arts Museums of San Francisco, California

1997 *20th Anniversaire du Centre National d'Art et de Culture*
Centre Georges Pompidou, Paris, France

1996 *Continuity and Contradiction: A New Look at the Permanent Collection*
Museum of Contemporary Art, San Diego, California

Abstraction in the Twentieth Century: Total Risk, Freedom, Discipline
Solomon R. Guggenheim Museum, New York, New York

1995 *Views from Abroad: European Perspectives on American Art I*
Whitney Museum of American Art, New York, New York. Traveled to Stedelijk Museum, Amsterdam, The Netherlands

Made in America: Ten Centuries of American Art
The Minneapolis Institute of Arts, Minnesota. Traveled to The Saint Louis Art Museum, Missouri; Toledo Museum of Art, Ohio; The Nelson-Atkins Museum of Art, Kansas City, Missouri; and Carnegie Museum of Art, Pittsburgh, Pennsylvania

pages 42-43 *Blue Black Red Green,* 2000
Oil on canvas (4 separate panels),
100 x 484 ½ inches overall

Josiah McElheny

Born 1966 in Boston, Massachusetts. Lives and works in New York, New York.

1988 Rhode Island School of Design,
Providence, Rhode Island, B.F.A.

Represented by **Brent Sikkema,** New York, New York,
and **Donald Young Gallery,** Chicago, Illinois

Selected Solo Exhibitions

2001 *Works: 1994-2000*
Johnson County Community College Gallery of
Art, Kansas City, Kansas

2000 *Christian Dior, Jorge Luis Borges, Adolf Loos*
Donald Young Gallery, Chicago, Illinois

Brent Sikkema, New York, New York

1999 *An Historical Anecdote About Fashion*
Henry Art Gallery, Faye G. Allen Center for the
Visual Arts, University of Washington—Seattle

The Story of Glass
Isabella Stewart Gardner Museum, Boston,
Massachusetts

1997 *Non-Decorative Beautiful Objects*
AC Project Room, New York, New York

Three Alter Egos
Donald Young Gallery, Seattle, Washington

1996 Barbara Krakow Gallery, Boston, Massachusetts

1995 Stephen Friedman Gallery, London, England

1994 *Authentic History*
The Robert Lehman Gallery of the New York
Experimental Glass Workshop, Brooklyn, New York

1993 *originals, fakes, reproductions*
William Traver Gallery, Seattle, Washington

1990 *Jägarens Glasmuseet*
The Hunter's Glass Museum, permanent
installation, Arnescruv, Sweden

Selected Group Exhibitions

2001 *Body Space*
The Baltimore Museum of Art,
Maryland

2000 *Exhibition Room*
Real Art Ways, Hartford, Connecticut

From Here to There
Schloss Solitude, Stuttgart, Germany

Whitney Biennial
Whitney Museum of American Art, New York,
New York

1998 *Young Americans, Part II*
The Saatchi Gallery, London, England

At Home in the Museum
The Art Institute of Chicago, Illinois

Personal Touch
Art in General, New York, New York

Interlacings
Whitney Museum of American Art at
Champion, Stamford, Connecticut

Inglenook
Feigen Contemporary, New York, New York,
and Illinois State University, Normal

1996 *A Labor of Love*
New Museum of Contemporary Art, New York,
New York

1995 *For Victoria* (with Dan Peterman)
Andrea Rosen Gallery, New York, New
York, and Grazer Kunstverein, Graz, Austria

VER-RÜCKT
Kulturstiftung Schloss Agathenburg,
Germany. Traveled to Museumsverein
Arolsen, Germany

pages 50-51 *Kärntner Bar, Vienna, 1908,
Adolf Loos (White)*, 2001
Installation with architectural details
and electric lighting
Room dimensions: 12 x 14 x 27 feet

Room includes:
*Bar Glass, Adolf Loos vs. Josef Hoffman
and Oswald Haerdtl, Vienna (White)*, 2001
Display cases, electric lighting, blown glass

*"Ornament and Crime," 1908,
Adolf Loos (White)*, 2001
Screen print

*American Flag at the Kärntner Bar,
Vienna, 1908, Adolf Loos (White)*, 2001
Glass and metal sign

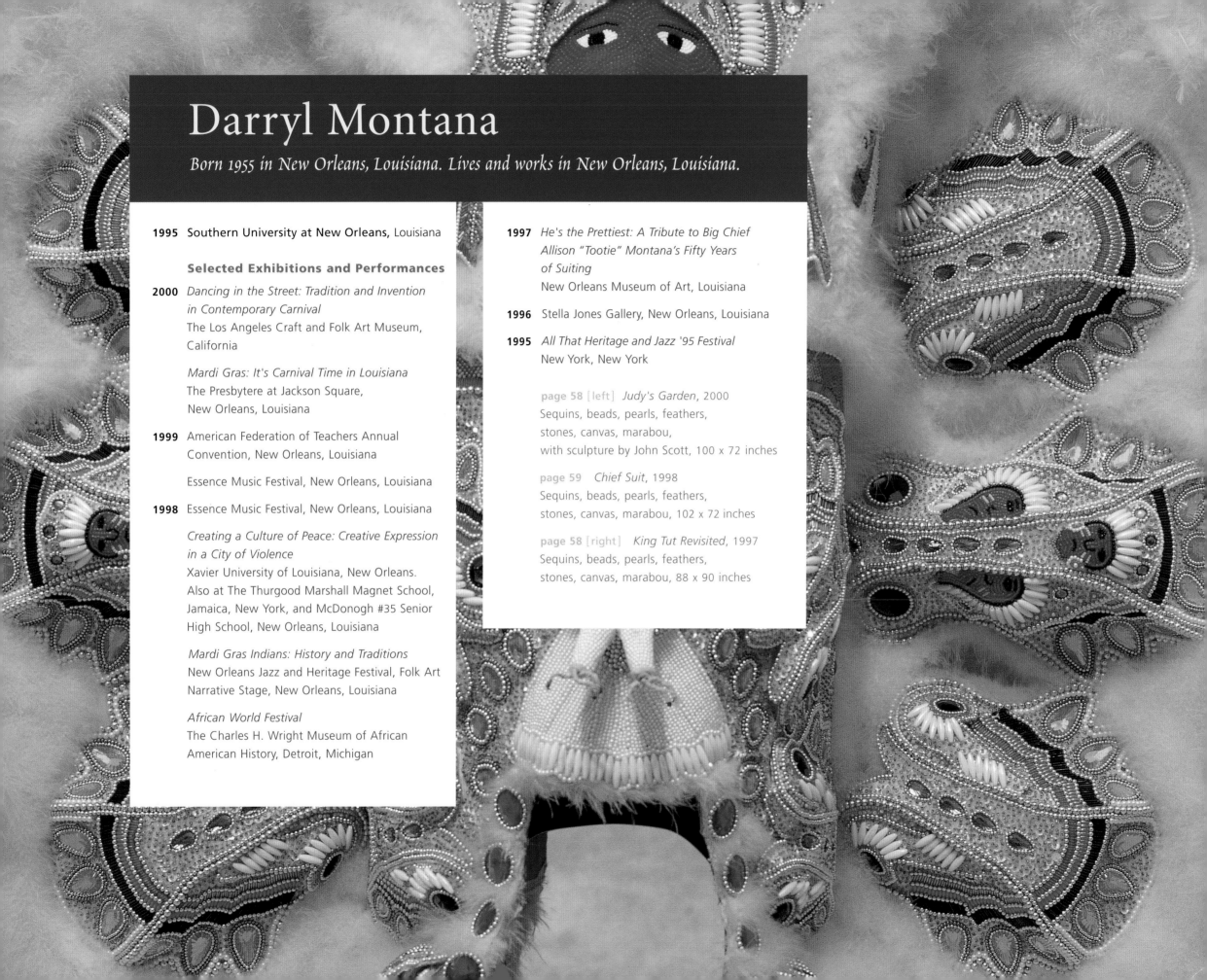

Darryl Montana

Born 1955 in New Orleans, Louisiana. Lives and works in New Orleans, Louisiana.

1995 Southern University at New Orleans, Louisiana

Selected Exhibitions and Performances

2000 *Dancing in the Street: Tradition and Invention in Contemporary Carnival*
The Los Angeles Craft and Folk Art Museum, California

Mardi Gras: It's Carnival Time in Louisiana
The Presbytere at Jackson Square,
New Orleans, Louisiana

1999 American Federation of Teachers Annual Convention, New Orleans, Louisiana

Essence Music Festival, New Orleans, Louisiana

1998 Essence Music Festival, New Orleans, Louisiana

Creating a Culture of Peace: Creative Expression in a City of Violence
Xavier University of Louisiana, New Orleans.
Also at The Thurgood Marshall Magnet School, Jamaica, New York, and McDonogh #35 Senior High School, New Orleans, Louisiana

Mardi Gras Indians: History and Traditions
New Orleans Jazz and Heritage Festival, Folk Art Narrative Stage, New Orleans, Louisiana

African World Festival
The Charles H. Wright Museum of African American History, Detroit, Michigan

1997 *He's the Prettiest: A Tribute to Big Chief Allison "Tootie" Montana's Fifty Years of Suiting*
New Orleans Museum of Art, Louisiana

1996 Stella Jones Gallery, New Orleans, Louisiana

1995 *All That Heritage and Jazz '95 Festival*
New York, New York

page 58 [left] *Judy's Garden*, 2000
Sequins, beads, pearls, feathers,
stones, canvas, marabou,
with sculpture by John Scott, 100 x 72 inches

page 59 *Chief Suit*, 1998
Sequins, beads, pearls, feathers,
stones, canvas, marabou, 102 x 72 inches

page 58 [right] *King Tut Revisited*, 1997
Sequins, beads, pearls, feathers,
stones, canvas, marabou, 88 x 90 inches

Sarah Morris

Born 1967 in Kent, England (American). Lives and works in New York and London, England.

1990 Whitney Museum of American Art
Independent Study Program, New York,
New York

1989 Brown University, Providence, Rhode Island, B.A.

Represented by **Friedrich Petzel Gallery,** New York,
New York; **Jay Jopling/White Cube,** London, England;
and **Galerie Max Hetzler,** Berlin, Germany

Selected Solo Exhibitions

2002 Palais de Tokyo, Paris, France

2001 *Correspondence*
Nationalgalerie im Hamburger Bahnhof,
Museum für Gegenwart, Berlin, Germany

      Friedrich Petzel Gallery, New York, New York

2000 Kunsthalle Zürich, Switzerland

      Philadelphia Museum of Art, Pennsylvania

      Galerie für Zeitgenössische Kunst,
Leipzig, Germany

      Rumjungle
White Cube², London, England

1999 Museum of Modern Art, Oxford, England

1998 Le Consortium, Centre D'Art Contemporain,
Dijon, France

1996 *One False Move*
White Cube, London, England

1993 *Sarah Morris*
Close-Up, New York, New York

1992 *Citizens*
New York Kunsthalle, New York

Selected Group Exhibitions

2001 *Hybrids: International Contemporary Painting*
Tate Liverpool, England

      Comfort: Reclaiming Place in a Virtual World
Cleveland Center for Contemporary Art, Ohio

2000 *Twisted: Urban and Visionary Landscapes
in Contemporary Painting*
Stedelijk Van Abbemuseum, Eindhoven,
The Netherlands

      The Song of the Earth
Museum Fridericianum, Kassel, Germany

      Confusion
Nationalgalerie im Hamburger Bahnhof,
Museum für Gegenwart, Berlin, Germany

      *What if: Art on the Verge of Architecture
and Design*
Moderna Museet, Stockholm, Sweden

1999 *Le Capital*
Centre Régional d'Art Contemporain, Sète, France

      Concrete Ashtray
Friedrich Petzel Gallery, New York, New York

      Frieze
The Institute of Contemporary Art,
Boston, Massachusetts

1998 *I Love New York*
Museum Ludwig, Cologne, Germany

1997 *Hospital* (organized by Sarah Morris)
Galerie Max Hetzler, Berlin, Germany

pages 108-109 *AM/PM*, 1999
16 mm film/DVD, 12 minutes, 36 seconds

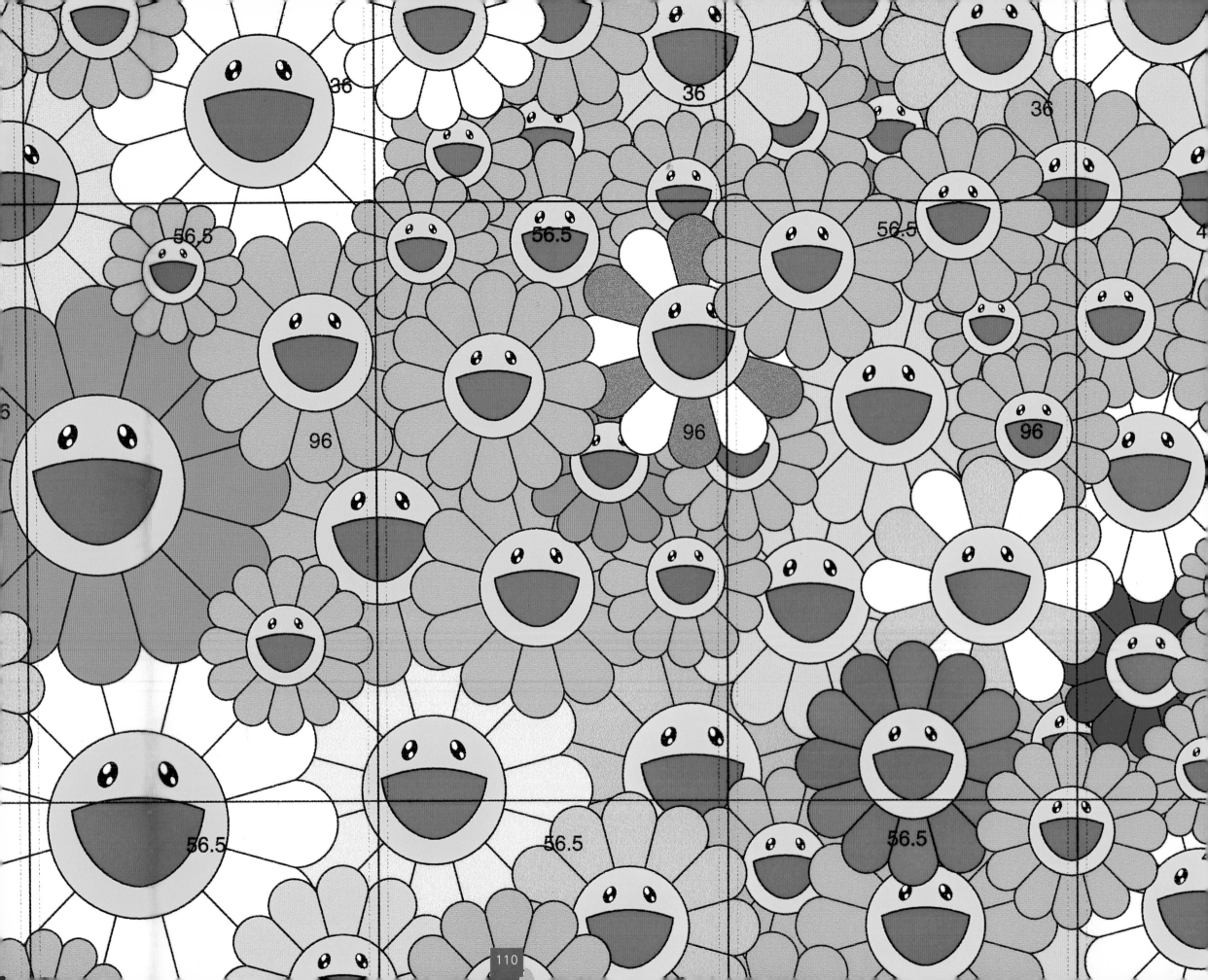

Takashi Murakami

Born 1962 in Tokyo, Japan. Lives and works in Saitama, Japan, and Brooklyn, New York.

1993 Tokyo National University of Fine Arts
and Music, Japan, Ph.D.
1988 Tokyo National University of Fine Arts
and Music, Japan, M.F.A.
1986 Tokyo National University of Fine Arts
and Music, Department of Traditional Japanese
Painting (*Nihon-ga*), Japan, B.F.A.

Represented by **Blum & Poe Gallery**, Los Angeles,
California; **Marianne Boesky Gallery**, New York,
New York; and **Tomio Koyama Gallery**, Tokyo, Japan

Selected Solo Exhibitions

2001 *Takashi Murakami*
Fondation Cartier pour l'art contemporain,
Paris, France

Takashi Murakami
Museum of Contemporary Art, Tokyo, Japan

Takashi Murakami: Made in Japan
Museum of Fine Arts, Boston, Massachusetts

2000 *Takashi Murakami: Second Mission Project K02*
P.S.1 Contemporary Art Center, Long Island City,
New York

1999 *Takashi Murakami: The Meaning of the Nonsense
of the Meaning*
Center for Curatorial Studies Museum, Bard
College, Annandale-on-Hudson, New York

Takashi Murakami: DOB in the Strange Forest
Parco Gallery, Tokyo, Japan

1998 *Back Beat*
Blum & Poe Gallery, Los Angeles, California

1996 *Takashi Murakami: Sculpture and Paintings*
Feature Inc., New York, New York

Takashi Murakami: 727
Tomio Koyama Gallery, Tokyo, Japan

1994 *Which is Tomorrow? - Fall in Love -*
SCAI the Bathhouse, Tokyo, Japan

1993 *Takashi Murakami: A Very Merry Unbirthday!*
Hiroshima City Museum of Contemporary Art,
Japan

1992 *Wild, Wild*
Rontgen Kunst Institut von Katsuya Ikeuchi
Gallery AG, Tokyo, Japan

1991 *Takashi Murakami*
(Doctor of Fine Arts Final Exhibition)
Art Gallery at Tokyo National University of
Fine Arts and Music, Japan

Selected Group Exhibitions

2001 *Painting at the Edge of the World*
Walker Art Center, Minneapolis, Minnesota

Superflat (curated by Takashi Murakami)
The Museum of Contemporary Art, Los
Angeles, California. Traveled to Walker Art
Center, Minneapolis, Minnesota, and Henry Art
Gallery, Faye G. Allen Center for the Visual
Arts, University of Washington—Seattle

2000 *Twisted: Urban and Visionary Landscapes in
Contemporary Painting*
Stedelijk Van Abbemuseum, Eindhoven,
The Netherlands

Let's Entertain
Walker Art Center, Minneapolis, Minnesota.
Traveled to Portland Art Museum, Oregon;

Musée national d'art Moderne, Centre
Georges Pompidou, Paris, France;
Kunstmuseum Wolfsburg, Germany;
Museo Rufino Tamayo, Mexico City, Mexico;
and The Saint Louis Art Museum, Missouri

5th Biennale d'Art Contemporain de Lyon
France

1999 *53rd Carnegie International*
Carnegie Museum of Art, Pittsburgh,
Pennsylvania

Colour me blind!
Württembergischer Kunstverein Stuttgart,
Germany

1997 *Ero Pop Tokyo* (curated by Takashi Murakami)
George's, Los Angeles, California

1996 *Tokyo Pop*
The Hiratsuka Museum of Art, Kanagawa,
Japan

1995 *Venice Biennale*
Italy

Japan Today
Louisiana Museum of Modern Art,
Humlebaek, Denmark; Kunstnernes Hus,
Oslo, Norway; Liljevalchs Konsthall,
Stockholm, Sweden; and Wäinö Aaltonen
Museum of Art, Turku, Finland

1992 *Anomaly*
Rontgen Kunst Institut, Tokyo, Japan

page 48 *Hyakki-Yagyou*, 2001
Vinyl, helium, lead, Corian,
adhesive-backed mural
Rotunda dimensions: 18½ x 15 x 7½ feet

Nic Nicosia

Born 1951 in Dallas, Texas. Lives and works in Dallas, Texas.

1974 **University of North Texas,** Denton, B.A.

Represented by **Dunn and Brown Contemporary,**
Dallas, Texas, and **P.P.O.W.,** New York, New York

Selected Solo Exhibitions

2000 *Movies 1997-1999*
P.P.O.W., New York, New York

1999 *Real Pictures 1979-1999*
Contemporary Arts Museum, Houston, Texas.
Traveled to Dallas Museum of Art, Texas, and
Cleveland Center for Contemporary Art, Ohio

1997 *Acts and Sex Acts*
P.P.O.W., New York, New York

1996 *Nic Nicosia*
Richard Foncke Gallery, Gent, Belgium

1993 *Love + Lust*
Raab Gallery, London, England

Linda Cathcart Gallery, Santa Monica, California

1991 *Love + Lust*
Pace/MacGill Gallery, New York, New York

1988 *Real Pictures*
Bruno Facchetti Gallery, New York, New York

1987 Honolulu Academy of Arts, Hawaii

1986 *Concentrations 13 — Nic Nicosia*
Dallas Museum of Art, Texas

1985 *Nic Nicosia's Realities*
Milwaukee Art Museum, Wisconsin

1982 Artists Space, New York, New York

Selected Group Exhibitions

2000 *Whitney Biennial*
Whitney Museum of American Art, New York,
New York

1998 *7th New York Video Festival*
Walter Reade Theater, New York, New York

1994 *Family Lives*
Corcoran Gallery of Art, Washington, D.C.

1992 *Documenta IX*
Kassel, Germany

1991 *Pleasures and Terrors of Domestic Comfort*
The Museum of Modern Art, New York,
New York

1989 *Konstruiete Fotografie*
Kunstverein München, Munich, Germany.
Traveled in Germany to Kunsthalle Nürnberg;
Forum Böttcheesta Be, Bremen; and Badischer
Kunstverein, Karlsruhe

1987 *Arrangements for the Camera:
A View of Contemporary Photography*
The Baltimore Museum of Art, Maryland

Torino Fotografia '87
International Biennial of Photography,
Torino, Italy

The New Photography
Contemporary Arts Museum, Houston, Texas

1983 *Whitney Biennial*
Whitney Museum of American Art, New York,
New York

Image Fabrique
Musée national d'art Moderne, Centre
Georges Pompidou, Paris, France

*New Perspectives in American Art:
1983 Exxon National Exhibition*
Solomon R. Guggenheim
Museum, New York, New York

pages 112-113 *On Acting America*, 2001
16mm film transferred to DVD,
17 minutes, 49 seconds

Kermit Oliver

Born 1943 in Refugio, Texas. Lives and works in Waco, Texas.

1967 **Texas Southern University,** Houston, B.F.A.

Represented by **Hooks-Epstein Galleries, Inc.,** Houston, Texas

Selected Solo Exhibitions

1999 *Palimpsest*
Hooks-Epstein Galleries, Inc., Houston, Texas

1997 *Kermit Oliver: Painting, Texas Realists: Contemporary Artists Exhibition Series*
Museum of the Southwest, Midland, Texas

1991 Hooks-Epstein Galleries, Inc., Houston, Texas

1989 *Kermit Oliver: Current Allegories*
Art Museum of Southeast Texas, Beaumont. Traveled to The Art Center of Waco, Texas

1989 *New Works*
Hooks-Epstein Galleries, Inc., Houston, Texas

Kermit Oliver: Contemporary Allegories of the Mythical and the Spiritual
Austin Museum of Art (Laguna Gloria), Texas

1987 *Works on Paper*
Hooks-Epstein Galleries, Inc., Houston, Texas

Selected Group Exhibitions

2001 *The Box*
Hooks-Epstein Galleries, Inc., Houston, Texas

1996 *Intimate*
Barbara Davis Gallery (Pennzoil Place), Houston, Texas

New Beginnings
Hooks-Epstein Galleries, Inc., Houston, Texas

1995 *Texas Myths and Realities*
The Museum of Fine Arts, Houston, Texas

1994 *Texas Selections from the Collection*
Art Museum of Southeast Texas, Beaumont

Veiled Images
Art Museum of South Texas, Corpus Christi, Texas, and SFA Gallery, Stephen F. Austin State University, Nacogdoches, Texas

Landscape Without Figures
Hooks-Epstein Galleries, Inc., Houston, Texas

1993 *Texas Contemporaries: Acquisitions of the Nineties*
The Museum of Fine Arts, Houston, Texas

1990 *The Blues Aesthetic: Black Culture and Modernism*
Blaffer Gallery, University of Houston, Texas

Humphreys-Fentress Collection: American Artists
Wichita Falls Museum and Art Center, Texas

1985 *Fresh Paint: the Houston School*
The Museum of Fine Arts, Houston, Texas

1982 *The Figure Painting in American Art*
Contemporary Arts Center, New Orleans

page 37   *Tobias*, 1997
Acrylic on birch panel,
46 inches (diameter) x 3 inches

pages 114-115   *Polyphemus*, 1991
Acrylic on birch panel, 29 x 28¾ inches

page 38   *Pigs in a Radial Poke*, 1983
Acrylic on birch panel, 38 x 48 x 2 inches

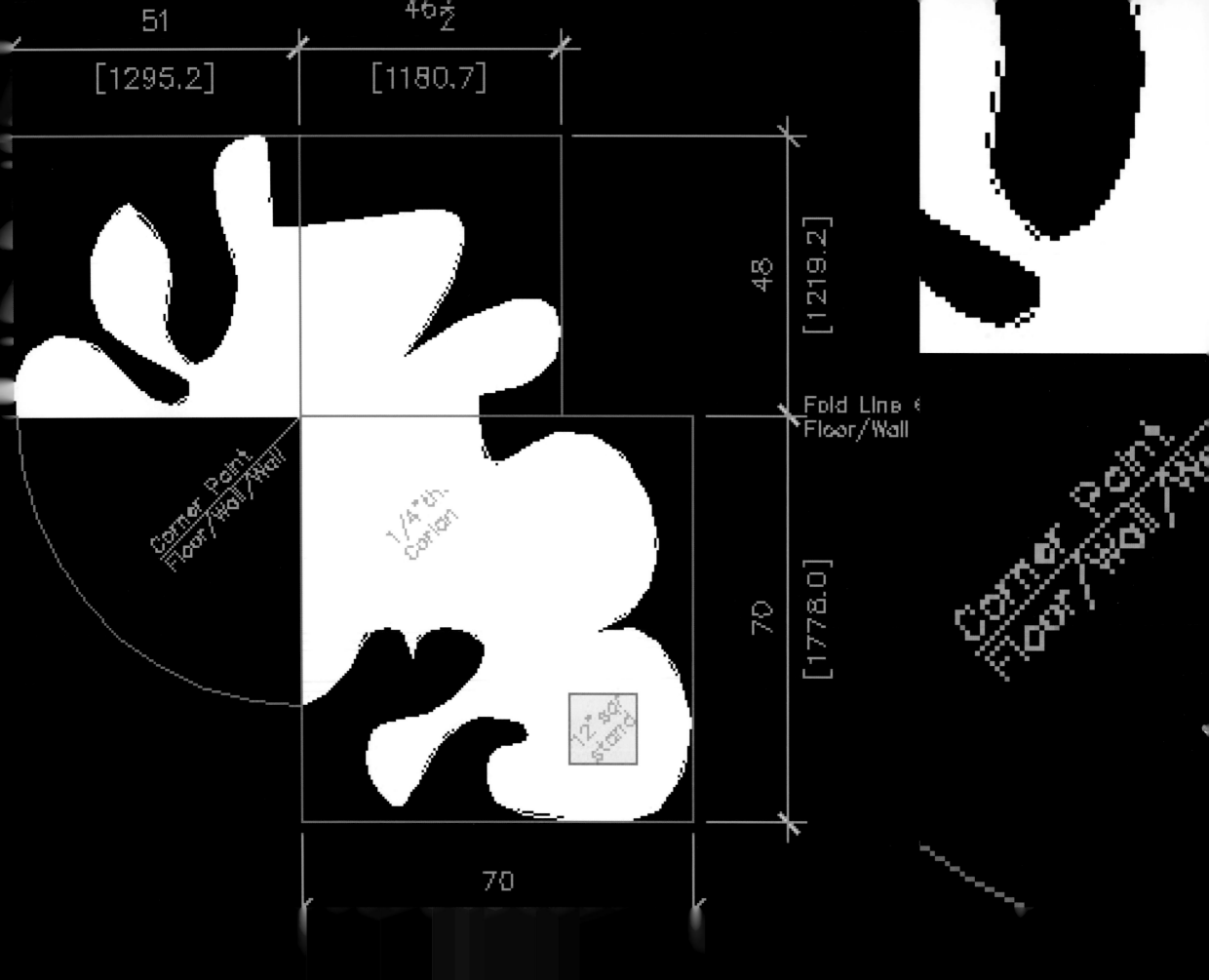

Jorge Pardo

Born 1963 in Havana, Cuba. Lives and works in Los Angeles, California.

Art Center College of Design, Pasadena, California, B.F.A.

Represented by **Friedrich Petzel Gallery,** New York, New York, and **1301PE,** Los Angeles, California

Selected Solo Exhibitions

2001 Friedrich Petzel Gallery, New York, New York

2000 Dia Center for the Arts, New York, New York

Kunsthalle Basel, Switzerland

1999 The Fabric Workshop and Museum, Philadelphia, Pennsylvania

Royal Festival Hall, London, England

neugerriemschneider, Berlin, Germany

1998 The Museum of Contemporary Art, Los Angeles, California

1997 *Lighthouse*
Museum Boijmans Van Beuningen, Rotterdam, The Netherlands

Museum of Contemporary Art, Chicago, Illinois

1994 *One Component of the Work Is That the Show Will Have Many Titles, One of Them Being: MoCA.Three Prints Per Second*
Friedrich Petzel/Nina Borgmann, New York, New York

1993 Person's Weekend Museum, Tokyo, Japan

Tom Solomon's Garage, Los Angeles, California

Selected Group Exhibitions

2001 *Public Offerings*
The Museum of Contemporary Art, Los Angeles, California

In Between: Art and Architecture
MAK Center for Art and Architecture, Los Angeles, California

Lens and Paper: The Louden Collection
Gemeentemuseum, The Hague, The Netherlands

2000 *Against Design*
Institute of Contemporary Art, University of Pennsylvania—Philadelphia; Palm Beach Institute of Contemporary Art, Lake Worth, Florida; Museum of Contemporary Art, San Diego, California; and Kemper Museum of Contemporary Art, Kansas City, Missouri

What if: Art on the Verge of Architecture and Design
Moderna Museet, Stockholm, Sweden

1997 *Kunst Arbeit*
Aus der Sammlung Sud West LB, Stuttgart, Germany

Rooms With a View: Environments for Videos
Solomon R. Guggenheim Museum, New York, New York

Skulptur. Projekte in Münster 1997
Münster, Germany

1996 *Defining the Nineties: Consensus Making in New York, Miami, and Los Angeles*
Museum of Contemporary Art, North Miami, Florida

Projekte/Projects: Art at the New Trade Fair of Leipzig
Leipzig, Germany

1994 *Pure Beauty: Some Recent Work from Los Angeles*
The Museum of Contemporary Art, Los Angeles, California. Traveled to American Center, Paris, France

pages 58-59 *BOO!*, 2001
3 Corian pedestals,
approximately 4 x 6 x 6 feet each

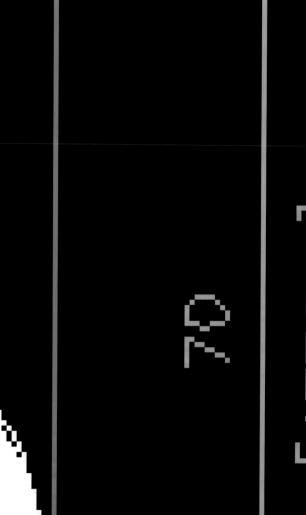

Ken Price

Born 1935 in Los Angeles, California. Lives and works in Venice, California, and Taos, New Mexico.

1959 New York State College of Ceramics
at Alfred University, Alfred, New York, M.F.A.
1957 Los Angeles County Art Institute, California
1956 University of Southern California,
Los Angeles, B.F.A.

Represented by **L.A. Louver Gallery**, Venice, California;
Franklin Parrasch Gallery, New York, New York;
Klein Art Works, Chicago, Illinois; and **James Kelly
Contemporary**, Santa Fe, New Mexico

Selected Solo Exhibitions

2001 Klein Art Works, Chicago, Illinois

L.A. Louver Gallery, Venice, California

1998 Franklin Parrasch Gallery, New York, New York

1992 The Menil Collection, Houston, Texas

Walker Art Center, Minneapolis, Minnesota

1983 Leo Castelli Gallery, New York, New York

1980 James Corcoran Gallery, Santa Monica, California

1978 *Happy's Curios*
Los Angeles County Museum of Art, California

1974 Willard Gallery, New York, New York

1969 Whitney Museum of American Art, New York,
New York

1968 Kasmin Gallery, London, England

1960 Berus Gallery, Los Angeles, California

Selected Group Exhibitions

2000 *Made in California: Art, Image,
and Identity, 1900-2000*
Los Angeles County Museum of Art, California

The Sixties: 1960-69
The Museum of Contemporary Art,
Los Angeles, California

1999 *Clay into Art: Selections from the
Contemporary Ceramics Collection*
The Metropolitan Museum of Art,
New York, New York

1998 *American Academy Invitational Exhibition
of Painting and Sculpture*
American Academy of Arts and Letters,
New York, New York

1997 *Sunshine & Noir: Art in Los Angeles,
1960-1997*
Louisiana Museum of Modern Art,
Humlebaek, Denmark. Traveled to Castello di
Rivoli, Museo d'Arte Contemporanea, Torino,
Italy; Hayward Gallery, London, England; Haus
der Kunst, Münich, Germany; and The UCLA
Hammer Museum, Los Angeles, California

1988 *Big/Little Sculpture*
Williams College Museum of Art,
Williamstown, Massachussetts

1984 *An International Survey of Recent Painting
and Sculpture*
The Museum of Modern Art, New York,
New York

1982 *Painting and Sculpture Today*
Indianapolis Museum of Art, Indiana

1981 *Ceramic Sculpture, Six Artists*
Whitney Museum of American Art,
New York, New York

1972 *West Coast, U.S.A.*
Kölnischer Kunstverein, Cologne, Germany

1966 *Robert Irwin/Kenneth Price*
Los Angeles County Museum of Art, California

1964 *New American Sculpture*
Pasadena Art Museum, California

page 44 [right] *Welsh*, 2001
Fired and painted clay, 21 x 19½ x 15¼ inches

page 45 [left] *Cheeks*, 1998
Fired and painted clay, 19 x 29½ x 16 inches

page 44 [left] *Underhung*, 1997
Fired and painted clay, 23½ x 21½ x 16 inches

page 45 [right] *Pagan*, 1996
Fired and painted clay, 26 x 22½ x 13½ inches

Stephen Prina

Born 1954 in Galesburg, Illinois. Lives and works in Los Angeles, California.

1980 **California Institute of the Arts,** Valencia, M.F.A.
1977 **Northern Illinois University,** DeKalb, B.F.A.
1974 **Carl Sandburg College,** Galesburg, Illinois, Associate of Arts

Represented by **Galerie Gisela Capitain**, Cologne, Germany; **Margo Leavin Gallery**, Los Angeles, California; and **Friedrich Petzel Gallery,** New York, New York

Selected Solo Exhibitions

2001 *What's wrong? Open the door! What's wrong? Open the door! ...I was scared. What happened? ...You can't lie underwater like on a bed and then just wait. You can't lie underwater like on a bed and just wait. ...It's impossible. ...Wait for what? Idiot! Do you know the mess you can get me into?*
Northern Illinois University Art Museum, Chicago

2000 *"It was the best he could do at the moment,"* reprise
ArtPace, San Antonio, Texas

To the People of Berlin
Hamburger Bahnhof and Freunde Guter Musik, Berlin, Germany

To the People of Frankfurt am Main: At Least Three Types of Inaccessibility
Frankfurter Kunstverein, Frankfurt am Main, Germany

1998 *2 or 3 Things I Know about Her (Second Investigation): Stephen Prina's Monochrome Painting*
Musée d'Art Moderne et Contemporain, Geneva, Switzerland

1996 *Retrospection Under Duress (Reprise)*
daadgalerie, Berlin, Germany

1992 *Beat of the Traps* (collaboration with Mike Kelley and Anita Pace)
Remise, Vienna, Austria, and University of Judaism, Los Angeles, California

"It was the best he could do at the moment"
Museum Boijmans Van Beuningen, Rotterdam, The Netherlands

1990 *Monochrome Painting*
P.S.1 Contemporary Art Center, Long Island City, New York

1989 *Monochrome Painting*
The Renaissance Society at the University of Chicago, Illinois

1988 *Stephen Prina*
University Art Museum, University of California—Santa Barbara

Selected Group Exhibitions

1992 *Documenta IX*
Kassel, Germany

Allegories of Modernism: Contemporary Drawing
The Museum of Modern Art, New York, New York

1991 *51st Carnegie International*
Carnegie Museum of Art, Pittsburgh, Pennsylvania

Beyond the Frame: American Art 1960-1990
Setagaya Art Museum, Tokyo, Japan. Traveled in Japan to The National Museum of Art, Osaka, and Fukuoka Art Museum

Feux pâles
Musée d'Art Contemporain, Bordeaux, France

1990 *Venice Biennale*
Italy

The Readymade Boomerang
The Biennale of Sydney, Australia

1989 *A Forest of Signs: Art in the Crisis of Representation*
The Museum of Contemporary Art, Los Angeles, California

Prospect 89
Schirn Kunsthalle and Frankfurter Kunstverein, Frankfurt am Main, Germany

1988 *The Binational: American Art of the Late '80s*
Institute of Contemporary Art and the Museum of Fine Arts, Boston, Massachusetts. Traveled to Städtische Kunsthalle, Kunstsammlung Nordrhein-Westfalen, and Kunstverein für die Rheinlande und Westfalen, Düsseldorf, Germany; Kunsthalle Bremen, Germany; National Art Gallery, Athens, Greece; Württembergischer Kunstverein Stuttgart, Germany; and Ateneum, The Finnish National Gallery, Helsinki

1985 *The Art of Memory/The Loss of History*
New Museum of Contemporary Art, New York, New York

1982 *74th American Exhibition*
The Art Institute of Chicago, Illinois

pages 120-121 *Vinyl II*, 2000
16 mm film, color/sound,
21 minutes, 30 seconds

Bridget Riley

Born 1931 in London, England. Lives and works in London, England.

1955 **Royal College of Art,** London, England
1952 **Goldsmiths College,** London, England

Represented by **Pace Wildenstein,** New York, New York, and **Karsten Schubert,** London, England

Selected Solo Exhibitions

2002 *Bridget Riley: Paintings and Studies 1981-2002*
Kaiser Wilhelm Museum and Museum Haus Esters, Krefeld, Germany

2000 *Bridget Riley: Reconnaissance*
Dia Center for the Arts, New York, New York

Bridget Riley: Paintings 1982-2000 and Early Works on Paper
Pace Wildenstein, New York, New York

Bridget Riley: New Paintings and Gouaches
Waddington Galleries, London, England

1999 *Bridget Riley: Paintings from the 1960s and '70s*
Serpentine Gallery, London, England

1994 *Bridget Riley: Six Paintings from 1963-'93*
Tate Gallery, London, England

1984 *Working with Colour: Recent Paintings and Studies by Bridget Riley*
Arts Council of Great Britain. Traveled in Great Britain to DLI Museum and Art Gallery, Durham; Huddersfield Art Gallery, Durham; Ferens Art Gallery, Hull; City Museum and Art Gallery, Stoke-on-Trent; Usher Gallery, Lincoln; Bristol City Museum and Art Gallery; Towner Art Gallery, Eastbourne; Norwich Castle Museum; Harris Museum and Art Gallery, Preston; York City Art Gallery; and Mappin Art Gallery, Sheffield

1978 *Bridget Riley: Works 1959-78*
British Council retrospective. Traveled to Albright-Knox Art Gallery, Buffalo, New York; Dallas Museum of Art, Dallas, Texas; Neuberger Museum of Art, Purchase, New York; Art Gallery of New South Wales, Sydney, Australia; Art Gallery of Western Australia, Perth; and The National Museum of Modern Art, Tokyo, Japan

1973 *Bridget Riley: Paintings and Drawings 1961-1973*
Arts Council of Great Britain. Traveled in Great Britain to The Whitworth Art Gallery, Manchester; Mappin Art Gallery, Sheffield; DLI Museum and Art Gallery, Durham; Scottish National Gallery of Modern Art, Edinburgh, Scotland; City Museum and Art Gallery, Birmingham; Letchworth Museum and Art Gallery; and City Art Gallery and Arnolfini Gallery, Bristol

1966 *Bridget Riley: Drawings*
The Museum of Modern Art, New York, New York

1965 *Bridget Riley*
Richard Feigen Gallery, New York, New York

1962 *Bridget Riley*
Gallery One, London, England

Selected Group Exhibitions

2000 *Collection 2000*
Tate Modern, London, England

1998 *White Noise*
Kunsthalle Bern, Switzerland

1993 *The Sixties Art Scene in London*
Barbican Art Gallery, London, England

1989 *The Experience of Painting: Eight Modern Artists*
South Bank Centre, London, England

1982 *Aspects of British Art Today*
Arts Council of Great Britain. Traveled in Japan to Tokyo Metropolitan Museum; Tochigi Prefectural Museum of Fine Arts; The National Museum of Art, Osaka; Fukuoka Art Museum; and Hokkaido Museum of Modern Art, Sapporo

1978 *Recent British Art*
British Council retrospective. Traveled to Albright-Knox Art Gallery, Buffalo, New York; Museum of Fine Arts, Dallas, Texas; Neuberger Museum, Purchase, New York; Centrepoint Gallery Space, Sydney, Australia; Art Gallery of Western Australia, Perth; and The National Museum of Modern Art, Tokyo, Japan

1974 *British Painting '74*
Hayward Gallery, London, England

1968 *New British Painting and Sculpture*
Organized by Whitechapel Art Gallery, London, United Kingdom

Venice Biennale
Italy

1965 *The Responsive Eye*
The Museum of Modern Art, New York, New York

1964 *Nouvelle Tendence*
Musée des Arts Décoratifs, Paris, France

The New Generation
Whitechapel Art Gallery, London, England

page 27 *Evoe 1,* 1999-2000
Oil on linen (2 panels),
76¼ x 228¼ inches overall

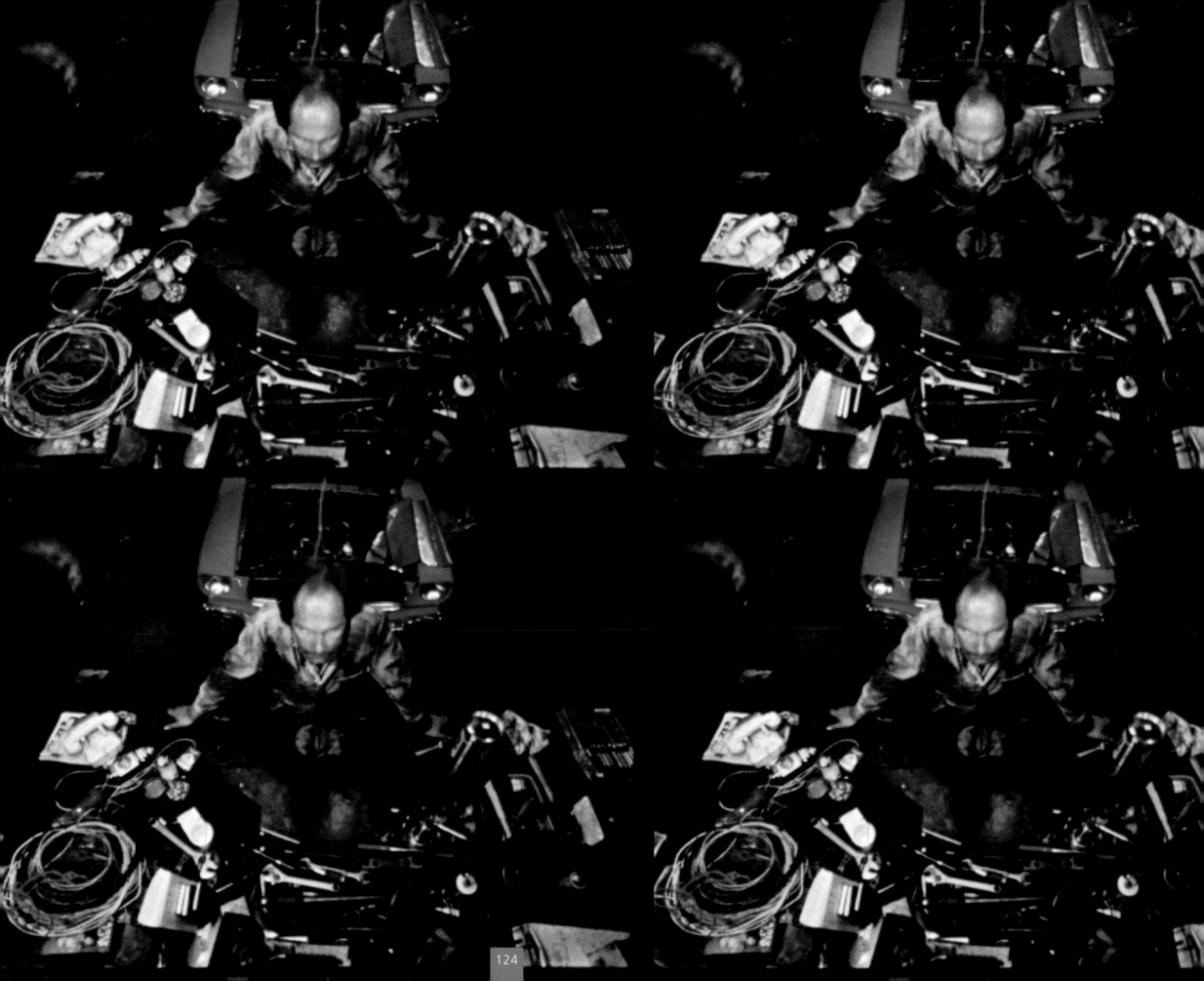

Ed Ruscha

Born 1937 in Omaha, Nebraska. Lives and works in Los Angeles, California.

1956- **Chouinard Art Institute,** Los Angeles,
1960 California

Represented by **Gagosian Gallery,** Los Angeles,
California, and New York, New York; and **Anthony
d'Offay Gallery,** London, England

Selected Solo Exhibitions

2000 *Ed Ruscha*
Hirshhorn Museum and Sculpture Garden
Washington, D.C. Traveled to the Museum of
Contemporary Art, Chicago, Illinois;
Miami Art Museum, Florida; Modern Art
Museum of Fort Worth, Texas; and Museum
of Modern Art, Oxford, England

Edward Ruscha: Editions 1959-1999
Walker Art Center, Minneapolis, Minnesota.
Traveled to Los Angeles County Museum of Art,
California; University of South Florida
Contemporary Art Museum, Tampa; and Austin
Museum of Art, Texas

Mountains and Highways
Anthony d'Offay Gallery, London, England

Powders, Pressures, and Other Drawings
John Berggruen Gallery, San Francisco, California

1998 *Retrospective of Works on Paper by
Edward Ruscha*
J. Paul Getty Museum, Los Angeles, California

1996 *VOWELS: Paintings on Book Covers*
Gagosian Gallery, Los Angeles, California

Camden Art Centre, London, England

1989 *Edward Ruscha, Paintings*
Musée national d'art Moderne, Centre
Georges Pompidou, Paris, France. Traveled to
Museum Boijmans Van Beuningen, Rotterdam,
The Netherlands; Fundació "la Caixa,"
Barcelona, Spain; Serpentine Gallery, London,
England; and The Museum of Contemporary
Art, Los Angeles, California

1982 *The Works of Ed Ruscha*
San Francisco Museum of Modern Art,
California. Traveled to Whitney Museum of
American Art, New York, New York; Vancouver
Art Gallery, Canada; San Antonio Museum of
Art, Texas; and Los Angeles County Museum
of Art, California

1976 Stedelijk Museum, Amsterdam, The Netherlands

1975 *Miracle*
Galerie Rolf Ricke, Cologne, Germany

1973 *Ed Ruscha/Drawings*
Leo Castelli Gallery, New York, New York

1969 La Jolla Museum of Art, California

1963 Ferus Gallery, Los Angeles, California

Selected Group Exhibitions

2000 *Quotidiana*
Castello di Rivoli, Museo d'Arte
Contemporanea, Torino, Italy

*How You Look At It — Photographs of the
20th Century*
Sprengel Museum, Hannover, Germany

1999 *The American Century: Art and Culture
1900-2000* (Part II, 1950-2000)
Whitney Museum of American Art, New York,
New York

53rd Carnegie International
Carnegie Museum of Art, Pittsburgh,
Pennsylvania

Heaven
Kunsthalle Düsseldorf, Germany.
Traveled to Tate Liverpool, England

1997 *Whitney Biennial*
Whitney Museum of American Art, New York,
New York

*Sunshine & Noir: Art in Los Angeles,
1960-1997*
Louisiana Museum of Modern Art,
Humlebaek, Denmark. Traveled to Castello di
Rivoli, Museo d'Arte Contemporanea, Torino,
Italy; Hayward Gallery, London, England; Haus
der Kunst, Münich, Germany; and The UCLA
Hammer Museum, Los Angeles, California

Venice Biennale
Italy

1992 *Documenta IX*
Kassel, Germany

1990 *High and Low: Modern Art and Popular
Culture*
The Museum of Modern Art, New York,
New York. Traveled to The Art Institute
of Chicago, Illinois, and The Museum of
Contemporary Art, Los Angeles, California

1987 *XXXth Anniversary – The First 15 Years: Part I*
Leo Castelli Gallery, New York, New York

1977 *A View of a Decade*
Museum of Contemporary Art, Chicago, Illinois

pages 124-125 *Miracle*, 1975
16mm film, 28 minutes

Alexis Smith

Born 1949 in Los Angeles, California. Lives and works in Venice, California.

1970 University of California—Irvine, B.A.

Represented by **Margo Leavin Gallery**, Los Angeles, California; **Artemis Greenberg Van Doren Gallery**, New York, New York; and **Modernism**, San Francisco, California

Selected Solo Exhibitions

2001 *An Embarrassment of Riches*
Artemis Greenberg Van Doren Gallery, New York, New York

2000 *The Sorcerer's Apprentice* (with Amy Gerstler)
Miami Art Museum, Florida

1999 *Words to Live By*
Margo Leavin Gallery, Los Angeles, California

1997 *My Favorite Sport*
Wexner Center for the Arts, Ohio State University, Columbus

A Matter of Taste
J. Paul Getty Museum, Los Angeles, California

1991 *Alexis Smith*
Whitney Museum of American Art, New York, New York. Traveled to The Museum of Contemporary Art, Los Angeles, California

1988 *On the Road*
Margo Leavin Gallery, Los Angeles, California

1987 *Same Old Paradise*
Brooklyn Museum of Art, New York, New York

1986 *Jane*
Walker Art Center, Minneapolis, Minnesota

1981 *U.S.A.*
Holly Solomon Gallery, New York, New York

1975 *Alexis Smith*
Whitney Museum of American Art, New York, New York

Selected Group Exhibitions

2001 *Postmodern Americans: A Selection*
The Menil Collection, Houston, Texas

2000 *Made in California: Art, Image, and Identity, 1900-2000*
Los Angeles County Museum of Art, California

1997 *Sunshine & Noir: Art in Los Angeles 1960-1997*
Louisiana Museum of Modern Art, Humlebaek, Denmark. Traveled to Castello di Rivoli, Museo d'Arte Contemporanea, Torino, Italy; Hayward Gallery, London, England; Haus der Kunst, Münich, Germany; and The UCLA Hammer Museum, Los Angeles, California

1996 *Blurring the Boundaries: Installation Art 1970-1996*
Museum of Contemporary Art, San Diego, California. Traveled to Memorial Art Gallery, Rochester, New York; Worcester Art Museum, Massachusetts; Ringling Museum of Art, Sarasota, Florida; Scottsdale Museum of Contemporary Art, Arizona; Davenport Museum of Art, Iowa; University of Texas, Austin; and San Jose Museum of Art, California

1995 *Art Works: The PaineWebber Collection of Contemporary Masters*
Museum of Fine Arts, Houston, Texas. Traveled to The Detroit Institute of Arts,

Michigan; Museum of Fine Arts, Boston, Massachusetts; The Minneapolis Institute of Arts, Minnesota; San Diego Museum of Art, California; Center for the Fine Arts, Miami, Florida; and Carnegie Museum of Art, Pittsburgh, Pennsylvania

1989 *Image World: Art and Media Culture*
Whitney Museum of American Art, New York, New York

1987 *Avant-Garde in the Eighties*
Los Angeles County Museum of Art, California

1986 *Individuals: A Selected History of Contemporary Art 1945-1986*
The Museum of Contemporary Art, Los Angeles, California

1984 *An International Survey of Recent Painting and Sculpture*
The Museum of Modern Art, New York, New York

1983 *Directions*
Hirshhorn Museum and Sculpture Garden, Washington D.C.

1977 *Paris Biennale*
Musee d'art Moderne, Paris, France

1975 *Whitney Biennial*
Whitney Museum of American Art, New York, New York

page 19 *Red Carpet*, 2001
Mixed-media installation with landscape wall painting and hand-tufted, New Zealand-wool area rug
Rug dimensions: 25 feet x 34 ½ feet x ½ inch

Jesús Rafael Soto

Born 1923 in Ciudad Bolívar, Venezuela. Lives and works in París, France, and Caracas, Venezuela.

1947 Escuela de Bellas Artes de Caracas, Venezuela

Represented by **Riva Yares Gallery**, Santa Fe, New Mexico, and Scottsdale, Arizona; **Galerie Denise René**, Paris, France; and **Galería de Arte Ascaso**, Valencia, Venezuela

Selected Solo Exhibitions

1998 Riva Yares Gallery, Scottsdale, Arizona

1997 Galerie Nationale du Jeu de Paume, Paris, France

1990 The Museum of Modern Art, Kamakura, Japan

1982 Palacio de Velázquez, Madrid, Spain

1979 Musée national d'art Moderne, Centre Georges Pompidou, Paris, France

1975 Hirshhorn Museum and Sculpture Garden, Washington, D.C.

1974 Solomon R. Guggenheim Museum, New York, New York

1970 Galerie Denise René, Paris, France

1969 Stedelijk Museum, Amsterdam, The Netherlands

Marlborough-Gerson Gallery, New York, New York

1968 Kunstverein für die Rheinlande und Westfalen, Düsseldorf, Germany

1957 Museo de Bellas Artes, Caracas, Venezuela

Selected Group Exhibitions

2000 *Heterotopías — Medio Siglo Sin-Lugar, 1918-1968*
Museo Nacional Centro de Arte Reina Sofía, Madrid, Spain

Campos de Fuerzas, un Ensayo sobre el Cinético
Museu d'Art Contemporàni de Barcelona, Spain. Traveled to Hayward Gallery, London, England

1992 *L'Art en Mouvement*
Fondation Maeght, Saint-Paul de Vence, France

1988 *15 Masters of Contemporary Sculpture*
Hyundai Gallery, Seoul, South Korea

1985 *Contrasts of Form: Geometric Abstract Art 1910-1980 from the Guggenheim Museum and The Museum of Modern Art, New York*
Biblioteca Nacional de España, Madrid, Spain. Traveled to Museo Nacional de Bellas Artes, Buenos Aires, Argentina; Museu de Arte de São Paulo Assis Chateaubriand, Brazil; and Museo de Arte Contemporáneo, Caracas, Venezuela

1984 *Ein Anderes Klima*
Städtische Kunsthalle, Düsseldorf, Germany

1965 *The Emergent Decade*
Andrew D. White Museum, Cornell University, Ithaca, New York. Traveled to the Dallas Museum of Art, Texas; the National Gallery of Canada, Ottawa; and Solomon R. Guggenheim Museum, New York, New York

1964 *Venice Biennale*
Italy

Bienal Americana de Arte
Córdoba, Argentina

1963 *Bienal de São Paulo*
Brazil

1961 *Bewogen Beweging*
Stedelijk Museum, Amsterdam, The Netherlands. Traveled to Moderna Museet, Stockholm, Sweden, and Louisiana Museum of Modern Art, Humlebaek, Denmark

1955 *Le Mouvement*
Galerie Denise René, Paris, France

page 57 *Grand écriture noire*, 1979
Acrylic on wood with metal,
98½ x 236½ inches

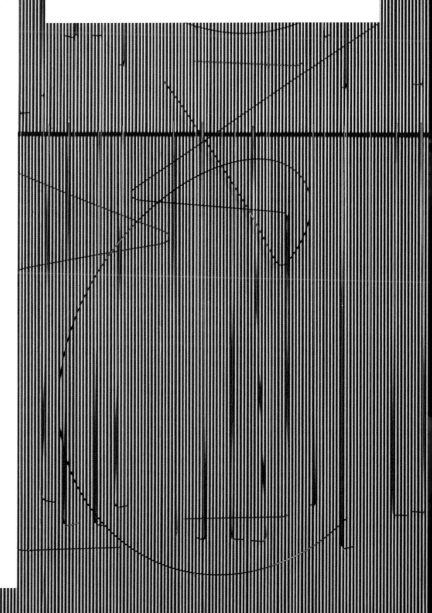

Jennifer Steinkamp and Jimmy Johnson

Jennifer Steinkamp born 1958 in Denver, Colorado. Jimmy Johnson born 1969 in Evanston, Illinois.

Jennifer Steinkamp

Lives and works in Los Angeles, California

1991 Art Center College of Design,
Pasadena, California, M.F.A.
1989 Art Center College of Design,
Pasadena, California, B.F.A.
1984 California Institute of the Arts, Valencia

Represented by **ACME.**, Los Angeles, California, and **Greengrassi Gallery,** London, England

Jimmy Johnson

Lives and works in Los Angeles, California

1990 New World School of the Arts, Miami, Florida
1989 Florida State University, Tallahassee,
Certificate in music composition
1987 North Carolina School of the Arts,
Winston Salem

Has released music with various labels under the name Grain.

Jennifer Steinkamp
Selected Solo Exhibitions

2001 Rice University Art Gallery, Houston, Texas

2000 *They Eat Their Wounded*
ACME., Los Angeles, California (soundtrack by Jimmy Johnson)

Aria
Fremont Street Experience, Las Vegas, Nevada (soundtrack by Jimmy Johnson)

Stiffs
Alyce de Roulet Williamson Gallery, Art Center College of Design, Pasadena, California (soundtrack by Jimmy Johnson)

1999 *X-Ray Eyes*
Staples Center, Los Angeles, California

Phase=Time
Henry Art Gallery, Faye G. Allen Center for the Visual Arts, University of Washington—Seattle (soundtrack by Jimmy Johnson)

Space Ghost
Greengrassi Gallery, London, England (soundtrack by Jimmy Johnson)

1998 *A Sailor's Life is a Life for Me*
ACME., Los Angeles, California (soundtrack by Jimmy Johnson)

1997 *Happy Happy*
Bravin Post Lee, New York, New York (soundtrack by Grain)

1995 *Smoke Screen*
Museum of Contemporary Art, North Miami, Florida (soundtrack by Grain)

1993 FOOD HOUSE, Santa Monica, California

1989 *Gender Specific*
The Santa Monica Museum of Art, California, and Bliss House, Los Angeles, California

Selected Group Exhibitions

2001 *One Wall: A Video Series*
Orange County Museum of Art, Newport Beach, California

COLA 2001 (City of Los Angeles Individual Artist Fellowship Award)
Skirball Cultural Center, Los Angeles, California

2000 *The 46th Biennial Exhibition: Media/Metaphor*
Corcoran Gallery of Art, Washington, D.C.

Made in California: NOW
Los Angeles County Museum of Art, LACMALab, California (soundtrack by Jimmy Johnson)

Wonderland
The Saint Louis Art Museum, Missouri (soundtrack by Andrew Bucksbarg)

1999 *Videodrome*
New Museum of Contemporary Art, New York, New York (soundtrack by Jimmy Johnson)

Postmark: An Abstract Effect
SITE Santa Fe, New Mexico

1998 *Ultralounge: The Return of Social Space (with Cocktails)*
DiverseWorks, Houston, Texas (soundtrack by Andrew Bucksbarg). Traveled to University of South Florida Contemporary Art Museum, Tampa

Public Works–A Community Laboratory
The Santa Monica Museum of Art, California (soundtrack by Andrew Bucksbarg)

1996 *Just Past: The Contemporary in MoCA's Permanent Collection, 1975-96*
The Museum of Contemporary Art, Los Angeles, California (soundtrack by Bryan Brown)

Videonale 7
Bonner Kunstverein, Bonn, Germany

pages **16-17** *sin* (*time*), 2001
DVD projection, curved wall,
sound, 96 ½ x 312 x 96 ½ inches

132

Jessica Stockholder

Born 1959 in Seattle, Washington (Canadian / American). Lives and works in New Haven, Connecticut.

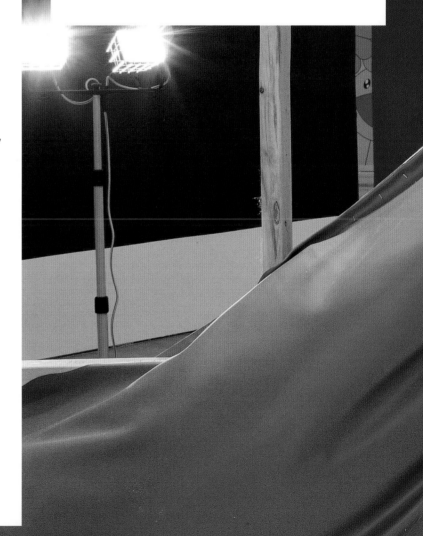

1985 Yale University, New Haven, Connecticut, M.F.A.
1982 University of Victoria, Canada, B.F.A.

Represented by **Gorney Bravin + Lee,** New York, New York; **Galerie Nächst St. Stephan,** Vienna, Austria; **Galerie Rolf Ricke,** Cologne, Germany; **Galleria Raffaella Cortese,** Milan, Italy; and **Galerie Nathalie Obadia,** Paris, France

Selected Solo Exhibitions

2001 Galerie Nächst St. Stephan, Vienna, Austria

Gorney Bravin + Lee, New York, New York

2000 Kunstmuseum St. Gallen, Switzerland

1999 The Power Plant, Toronto, Canada

1998 Openluchtmuseum voor beeldhouwkunst Middelheim, Antwerp, Belgium

Musée Picasso d'Antibes, France

Musée des Beaux-Arts de Nantes / La Salle Blanche, Nantes, France

1997 Kunstnernes Hus, Oslo, Norway

1995 Dia Center for the Arts, New York, New York

Fundació "la Caixa," Barcelona, Spain

1992 Westfälischer Kunstverein, Münster, Germany

1991 The Renaissance Society at The University of Chicago, Illinois

Selected Group Exhibitions

2000 *In the Beginning was MERZ*
Sprengel Museum, Hannover, Germany

Apparent Things: Painting with Things
Haus der Kunst München, Munich, Germany

1998 *Dijon / le Consortium.coll*
Musée national d'art Moderne,
Centre Georges Pompidou, Paris, France

Young Americans, Part II
Saatchi Gallery, London, England

1997 *Venice Biennale,*
Italy

1996 *Painting: The Extended Field*
Rooseum Center for Contemporary Art, Malmö, and Magasin 3 Stockholm Konsthall, Sweden

4th Biennale d'Art Contemporain de Lyon
France

1995 *Pittura - Immedia: Malerei in den 90er Jahren*
Neue Galerie am Landesmuseum Joanneum, Graz, Austria

1994 *Country Sculpture*
Le Consortium, Centre d'Art Contemporain, Dijon, France

Unbound: Possibilities in Painting
Hayward Gallery, London, England

1993 *As Long as It Lasts*
Witte de With, Rotterdam, The Netherlands

1991 *Whitney Biennial*
Whitney Museum of American Art, New York, New York

page 65   *Bird Watching,* 2001
Two couches, two urns, two benches, three lamps, light bulbs, wheelbarrow, wallpaper, carpet, control panels, hand truck, building materials, rocks, mirrors, rope, paint, and vinyl
Room dimensions: 14 ½ x 42 x 56 feet

Jane and Louise Wilson

Born 1967 in Newcastle, England. Live and work in London, England.

Jane Wilson
1992 Goldsmiths College, London, England, M.F.A.
1989 Newcastle Polytechnic, England, B.F.A.

Louise Wilson
1992 Goldsmiths College, London, England, M.F.A.
1989 Duncan of Jordanstone College of Art,
Dundee, Scotland, B.F.A.

Represented by **303 Gallery**, New York, New York, and
Lisson Gallery, London, England

Selected Two-Person Exhibitions
2000 *Star City & Proton, Unity, Energy, Blizzard*
303 Gallery, New York, New York

Parliament
Bernier/Eliades, Athens, Greece

Las Vegas, Graveyard Time
Dallas Museum of Art, Texas

1999 *The Turner Prize* (exhibition of shortlisted artists)
Tate Britain, London, England

Stasi City
Hamburger Kunsthalle, Hamburg, Germany

Jane and Louise Wilson
Serpentine Gallery, London, England

Gamma
Lisson Gallery, London, England

1998 *Stasi City*
303 Gallery, New York, New York

1997 *Stasi City*
Kunstverein Hannover, Germany. Traveled to
Kunstraum Munich, Germany; Centre d'Art
Contemporain, Geneva, Switzerland; and
Kunst-Werke, Berlin, Germany

1995 *Normapaths*
Chisenhale Gallery, London, England

Crawl Space
Milch Gallery, London, England

Selected Group Exhibitions
2001 *EGOFUGAL: Fugue from Ego for the Next
Emergence*
7th International Istanbul Biennial, Turkey

Public Offerings
The Museum of Contemporary Art,
Los Angeles, California

2000 *media_city seoul 2000*
Korean Biennial, Seoul, South Korea

*Age of Influence: Reflections in the Mirror of
American Culture*
Museum of Contemporary Art, Chicago,
Illinois

1999 *53rd Carnegie International*
Carnegie Museum of Art, Pittsburgh,
Pennsylvania

1997 *Pictura Britannica: Art from Britain*
Museum of Contemporary Art, Sydney,
Australia. Traveled to Art Gallery of South
Australia, Adelaide, and City Gallery,
Wellington, New Zealand

*Hyperamnesiac Fabulations:
The New British Art Scene*
The Power Plant, Toronto, Canada

1996 *Full House*
Kunstmuseum Wolfsburg, Germany

1995 *General Release*
British Council selection for *Venice Biennale*,
The Scuola San Pasquale, Venice, Italy

Wild Walls
Stedelijk Museum, Amsterdam,
The Netherlands

pages 134–135   *Dream time*, 2001
35mm film, 7 minutes, 11 seconds

Exhibition Checklist
Exhibition design by Dave Hickey and Graft Design

Kenneth Anger
pages 82-83
Kustom Kar Kommandos, 1965
16mm film, 3 minutes
Courtesy of the artist

Jo Baer
page 34
H. Arcuata, 1971
Oil on canvas, 22 x 96 x 4 inches
Courtesy of Paula Cooper Gallery,
New York, New York

V. Speculum, 1970
Oil on canvas, 80 x 22 x 4 inches
Courtesy of Paula Cooper Gallery,
New York, New York

Jeff Burton
page 55
Untitled #149 (upholstery tacks), 2001
Cibachrome print, 40 x 60 inches

pages 86-87
Untitled #156 (Fragonard), 2001
Cibachrome print, 40 x 60 inches

page 52
Untitled #126 (live to ride), 2000
Cibachrome print, 40 x 60 inches

page 47
Untitled #137 (globe), 2000
Cibachrome print, 40 x 60 inches

page 54
Untitled #48 (afghan), 1997
Cibachrome print, 60 x 40 inches

All work courtesy of the artist
and Casey Kaplan 10-6, New York,
New York. Partially commissioned
by SITE Santa Fe

James Lee Byars
pages 22-23
Eros, 1992
White Thassos marble (2 parts),
26¾ x 67 x 13½ inches overall
Courtesy of Michael Werner Gallery,
New York, New York, and
Cologne, Germany; and The
Estate of James Lee Byars

Pia Fries
page 26
quinto, 1994-95
Oil on wood (5 panels),
78¾ x 239⅜ inches overall
Courtesy of the artist; Mai 36
Galerie, Zürich, Switzerland; and
Galerie Rolf Ricke, Cologne, Germany

Gajin Fujita
pages 32-33
South Cali, 2001
Acrylic, spray paint, gold and silver
leaf on wood panel (12 panels),
48 x 192 x 2½ inches overall
Courtesy of Kravets/Wehby Gallery,
New York, New York, and
L.A. Louver Gallery, Venice, California.
Collection of Tom Strickler

Gajin Fujita with Alex Kizu
(K2SCrew) and **Jessie Simon**
(KGB Crew)
page 10
Graffiti Beau Monde, 2001
Spray paint, 24 x 100 feet
Commissioned by SITE Santa Fe

Graft Design
page 15
Kissy Kissy Touchy Touchy, 2001
Artificial flora, lava rocks, audio,
dimensions variable
Courtesy of the artists. Partially
commissioned by SITE Santa Fe

Frederick Hammersley
page 96
Side Saddle, 1979
Oil on canvas, 45 x 45 inches
Private Collection

page 25
Love Me, Love My Dog, 1972
Oil on canvas, 45 x 45 inches
Courtesy of the artist and
L.A. Louver Gallery, Venice,
California

Marine Hugonnier
page 49
Flower, 2000
Seasonal flowers, spray paint
for fresh flowers, vase,
dimensions variable
Courtesy of the artist and Galerie
Chantal Crousel, Paris, France.
Partially commissioned by SITE
Santa Fe

Jim Isermann
cover, pages 8-9
Untitled (*0101*) (*silver*), 2001
Painted vacuum formed ABS
plastic (750 panels), 24 x 24 x 3
inches each
Façade dimensions:
24 x 113 x 5½ feet
Courtesy of the artist;
Corvi-Mora, London, England;
Feature Inc., New York,
New York; and Richard Telles Fine
Art, Los Angeles, California.
Partially commissioned by
SITE Santa Fe

Ellsworth Kelly
pages 42-43
Blue Black Red Green, 2000
Oil on canvas (4 separate panels),
100 x 484½ inches overall
Courtesy of the artist
and Matthew Marks Gallery,
New York, New York

Josiah McElheny
pages 50-51
*Kärntner Bar, Vienna, 1908,
Adolf Loos* (*White*), 2001
Installation with
architectural details
and electric lighting
Room dimensions:
12 x 14 x 27 feet
Commissioned by SITE Santa Fe

Room includes:
*Bar Glass, Adolf Loos vs. Josef
Hoffman and Oswald Haerdtl, Vienna*
(*White*), 2001
Display cases, electric lighting, blown
glass

"*Ornament and Crime*," 1908, Adolf
Loos (*White*), 2001
Screen print

*American Flag at the Kärntner Bar,
Vienna, 1908,
Adolf Loos* (*White*), 2001
Glass and metal sign

Darryl Montana
page 58 [left]
Judy's Garden, 2000
Sequins, beads, pearls, feathers,
stones, canvas, marabou
with sculpture by John Scott,
100 x 72 inches
Courtesy of the artists

page 59
Chief Suit, 1998
Sequins, beads, pearls, feathers,
stones, canvas, marabou,
102 x 72 inches
Courtesy of the artist

page 58 [right]
King Tut Revisited, 1997
Sequins, beads, pearls, feathers,
stones, canvas, marabou,
88 x 90 inches
Courtesy of the artist

Sarah Morris
pages 108-109
AM/PM, 1999
16mm film/DVD,
12 minutes, 36 seconds
Courtesy of the artist;
Friedrich Petzel Gallery, New York,
New York; and Jay Jopling/White
Cube, London, England

Takashi Murakami
page 48
Hyakki-Yagyou, 2001
Vinyl, helium, lead, Corian,
adhesive-backed mural,
Rotunda dimensions:
18½ x 15 x 7½ feet
Courtesy of the artist
and Blum & Poe Gallery,
Los Angeles, California.
Partially commissioned
by SITE Santa Fe

Nic Nicosia
pages 112-113
On Acting America, 2001
16mm film transferred to DVD,
17 minutes, 49 seconds
Courtesy of the artist; Dunn and
Brown Contemporary, Dallas,
Texas; and P.P.O.W., New York,
New York

Kermit Oliver
page 37
Tobias, 1997
Acrylic on birch panel,
46 inches (diameter) x 3 inches
Courtesy of the artist and
Hooks-Epstein Galleries, Inc.,
Houston, Texas

pages 114-115
Polyphemus, 1991
Acrylic on birch panel,
29 x 28¾ inches
Private Collection

page 38
Pigs in a Radial Poke, 1983
Acrylic on birch panel,
38 x 48 x 2 inches
Private Collection

Jorge Pardo
pages 58-59
BOO!, 2001
3 Corian pedestals,
approximately 4 x 6 x 6 feet each
Commissioned by SITE Santa Fe

Ken Price
page 44 [right]
Welsh, 2001
Fired and painted clay,
21 x 19½ x 15¼ inches
Courtesy of the artist and L.A. Louver
Gallery, Venice, California

page 45 [left]
Cheeks, 1998
Fired and painted clay,
19 x 29½ x 16 inches
Private Collection

page 44 [left]
Underhung, 1997
Fired and painted clay,
23½ x 21½ x 16 inches
Courtesy of the artist and L.A. Louver
Gallery, Venice, California

page 45 [right]
Pagan, 1996
Fired and painted clay,
26 x 22½ x 13½ inches
Jackson Price Collection

Stephen Prina
pages 120-121
Vinyl II, 2000
16mm film, color/sound,
21 minutes, 30 seconds
Courtesy of the artist; Galerie Gisela
Capitain, Cologne, Germany; Margo
Leavin Gallery, Los Angeles,
California; and Friedrich Petzel
Gallery, New York, New York.
Commissioned for
Departures: 11 Artists at the Getty,
February 29 - May 7, 2000,
by the J. Paul Getty Museum,
Los Angeles, California

Bridget Riley
page 27
Evoe 1, 1999-2000
Oil on linen (2 panels),
76¼ x 228¼ inches overall
Courtesy of the artist and Karsten
Schubert, London, England

Ed Ruscha
pages 124-125
Miracle, 1975
16mm film, 28 minutes
Courtesy of the artist

Alexis Smith
page 19
Red Carpet, 2001
Mixed-media installation with land-
scape wall painting and hand-tufted,
New Zealand-wool area rug
Rug dimensions:
25 feet x 34½ feet x ½ inch
Commissioned by SITE Santa Fe

Jesús Rafael Soto
page 57
Grand écriture noire, 1979
Acrylic on wood with metal,
98½ x 236½ inches
Courtesy of the artist and
Riva Yares Gallery, Santa Fe, New
Mexico, and Scottsdale, Arizona

**Jennifer Steinkamp &
Jimmy Johnson**
pages 16-17
sin (time), 2001
DVD projection, curved wall, sound,
96½ x 312 x 96½ inches
Commissioned by SITE Santa Fe

Jessica Stockholder
page 65
Bird Watching, 2001
Two couches, two urns, two benches,
three lamps, light bulbs, wheelbarrow,
wallpaper, carpet, control panels,
hand truck, building materials, rocks,
mirrors, rope, paint, and vinyl
Room dimensions: 14½ x 42 x 56 feet
Commissioned by SITE Santa Fe

Jane & Louise Wilson
pages 134-135
Dream time, 2001
35mm film, 7 minutes, 11 seconds
Courtesy of the artists;
303 Gallery, New York,
New York; and Lisson Gallery,
London, England

Special Thanks

Major Contributors

The Andy Warhol Foundation for the Visual Arts, Anonymous, AT&T, The Board of Directors of SITE Santa Fe, The Brown Foundation, Inc., Houston, The Burnett Foundation, City of Santa Fe Arts Commission and the 1% Lodgers' Tax, Dunlevy Milbank Foundation, Inc., The Ford Foundation—New Directions/New Donors, The FUNd of Albuquerque Community Foundation, Agnes Gund and Daniel Shapiro, The Hearst Foundation, Inc., The Jodi Carson Memorial Fund, John D. and Catherine T. MacArthur Foundation, Emily Fisher Landau and Sheldon Landau, Lannan Foundation, LEF Foundation, LLWW Foundation, Anne and John Marion, The McCune Charitable Foundation, The Peter Norton Family Foundation, Philip Morris Companies Inc., Eliza Lovett Randall, Louisa Stude Sarofim, Sharp Electronics Corporation, SITE Unseen II Benefit Art Sale/James Kelly Contemporary, Sotheby's, Sotheby's International Realty

Additional Contributors

Appelbaum-Kahn Foundation, ART Santa Fe 2001, Frieda and Jim Arth, Penelope Arth and Peter Zavadil, ArtPace, Laura and Thomas Bacon, Mr. and Mrs. James Addison Baker, III, Gay Block and Malka Drucker, Brent Sikkema, Conlon Siegal Galleries, Frances Dittmer, Eagle Global Advisors, Étant Donnés—The French-American Fund for Contemporary Art, Bobbie Foshay-Miller and Chuck Miller, Gagosian Gallery, Katherine and James Gentry, Hotel Santa Fe (the official hotel of the Fourth International Biennial), Lili and Peter Knize, Nancy and Dr. Robert C. Magoon, Marlene Nathan Meyerson, Michael Werner, Inc., Alicia and William Miller, Ann and Ron Pizzuti, Caroline and Martin Proyect

In-Kind Contributors

Amanda's Flowers, *Art & Auction*, Frieda and Jim Arth, Bill Roth Plastering, Inc., The Black Hole, Copy Shack, DR Systems, Eclipse Production Services, Inc., The Flower Market, Jackalope Martin Sinkoff Wines, Inc., Mary Corley Antiques, Inc., Migs Pro Systems, Rental Service Corporation, Sam's Construction, Santa Fe Budget Inn, Staglin Family Wines, 303 Gallery, Voss Lighting, Walter Burke Catering

SITE Santa Fe is grateful to the following for their significant support of The Ford Foundation's New Directions/New Donors Challenge Grant

Bellas Artes
Deborah Berkman
Helen and Richard Brandt
Linda Durham Contemporary Art
Carolyn and Don Eason
Bobbie Foshay-Miller and
   Chuck Miller
Linda Hart Hermann and
   William Hermann
Ann Kippen and Louis Grachos, Jr.
Jeanne and Michael Klein
Toby Devan Lewis
The John D. and Catherine T.
   MacArthur Foundation
Susan and Lewis Manilow
Barbara and Donald Meyer
Sybil and Alfred J. Nadel
Barbara and Michael Ogg
Eliza Lovett Randall
Crennan and David Ray
Michael Robinson
Marcia Southwick and
   Murray Gell-Mann
The Eugene V. and
   Clare E. Thaw Charitable Trust
Jill & Donald Tishman

DIRECTOR'S ACKNOWLEDGMENTS

Yona Backer

Tom Beech

Susan Cahan

Sandy and Dr. Richard Carson

Christopher S. Chavez

Pamela Clapp

Christie Davis

Susan Emerling

Jaune Evans

Michael Friend

Jerry Ganguzza

Murray Gell-Mann

Barbara and Ray Graham

James Kelly

J. Patrick Lannan Jr.

Owen Lopez

Anne and John L. Marion

Jenée Misraje

James G. Niven

Eileen Norton

Peter Norton

Nancy Pittman

David M. Roche

Suzanne M. Sato

Kathleen Shields

CURATOR'S ACKNOWLEDGMENTS

Jim Arth

Linda Batkin

Douglas Baxter

Justine Birbil

Tim Blum

Alex Bradbury

David Burnhauser

Victoria Carlson

Annette Carlozzi

Walter Cassidy

Robert Christgau

Paula Cooper

Tommaso Corvi-Mora

Chiko

Chantal Crousel

Eric Davis

Turner Davis

Mary Dean

Dean Dedarko

Talley Dunn

Elizabeth East

Alvaro Erives

Arturo Erives

Bill Fagaly

Rebecca Friedman

Michael Friend

Jerry Ganguzza

Jay Gorney

Peter Gould

David Gregor and Irene Keil

Ed Grothius

Chris Heenan

Bill Hill

Rodney Hill

Geri Hooks

Fredericka Hunter

Lisa Ishikawa

Casey Kaplan

James Kelly

Jay Kobrin

Margo Leavin

Anne Livet

Libby Lumpkin

Mark McManus

Matthew Marks

Sam Martinez

Marlene Meyerson

Gordon Micunis

Sabrina Montana

Tootie Montana

Claire Munzenrider

Dave Olsen

David Pagel

Friedrich Petzel

Jeff Poe

Ann Powers

Happy Price

Chris Raab

David Reed

Bill Reynolds

Rolfe Ricke

Suzanne des Roches

Lisa Rosendahl

Louisa Stude Sarofim

Maureen Sarro

Randy Sommers

Karsten Schubert

Erin Shirreff

Brent Sikkema

Atelier Soto

Richard Telles

Mayo Thompson

Gordon Veneklassen

Nathalie Viot

Eva and Nick Walters

Mark Wehby

Dennis Yares

Riva Yares

Donald Young

SITE Santa Fe

Board of Directors

Joann Phillips
Honorary Chairman

Bobbie Foshay-Miller
President

John L. Marion
President Emeritus

William A. Miller
Treasurer

Marlene Nathan Meyerson
Secretary

Frieda Arth
Madelin Coit
James Fitzpatrick
Emily Fisher Landau
Nancy Magoon
Balene McCormick
Eliza Lovett Randall
Louisa Stude Sarofim
Dede Schuhmacher
A. Thomas Torres

Staff

Louis Grachos
Director & Curator

Emily Alsen
Head of Donor Relations
(through 10/2001)

Craig Anderson
Head of Exhibitions
Administration

Carlos Beuth
Facilities & Exhibitions
Assistant

Carol Cheh
Grant Writer* (as of 7/2001)

Kathryn Davis
Outreach and
Education Assistant*

Martha DeFoe
Visitor Services*

Julie Evanoff
Webmaster & Publications
Distribution

Rebecca Friedman
Editor and
Publications Coordinator*

Felicia Ponca
Office Manager (as of 7/2001)

Danielle Rae Miller
Development Assistant
& Membership
Coordinator

Chris Nail
Education Coordinator

Judith Podmore
Head of Education and
Outreach

Marita Prandoni
Assistant to the Director

Catherine Putnam
Head of Finance &
Administration

Ian Ramirez
Assistant to Exhibitions
and Curatorial*
(through 7/2001)

Wood Roberdeau
Office Manager
(through 7/2001)

Michelle Ryals
Accountant & Human
Resources

Erin Shirreff
Associate Curator
(through 9/2001)

Anne Blair Wrinkle
Public Relations &
Marketing Officer

*denotes part-time

Preparators

Jared Ashburn
Victoria Carlson
Krysten Cunningham
Patrick Day
Pam Ellison
Steve Fowler
Granville Greene
Michael Gurule
Austin Hanson
Tommy Harden
Roberto Hernandez
Paul Herrera
Corin Hewitt
James Holmes
William Hutchinson
Pat Kikut
Franky Kong
Laura McDannald
Rhonda Paynter
Lauro Perea
Carolyn Salas
Steven Sciscenti
Charles Sloan
Peter Sprunt
Matthew Szosz
James Van Soelen
Warren Wackman
Colin Zaug
Stephen Zolin

Projectionists

Molly Bradbury
Jesse Haas
Tommy Harden

Docents

Gretchen Berggren
Ali Cavanaugh
Madelin Coit
Carolyn Cook
Kathryn Davis
Ann Gaziano
Anne Hardin
Bill Hinsvark
Ja Soon Kim
Nancy Kriebel
Katrina Lasko
Susan Latham
Allan McMullen
Donald Meyer
Sally Mittler
John Mulvaney
Andrea Neff
Norma Ortega
Jennifer Schlesinger
Suki Shepard
Rusty Spicer
Signe Stuart
Sarah Tyson
Barbara Wilk
Judy Youens

Interns

Wynona S. Baca
Liz Batkin
David Ebeltoft
Amy Eldridge
Melissa Hordes
Mija Hübler
Megan Jacobs
Molly McGinnis
Rachel Montoya
Bess Murphy
Elisa Rosenberg
Claire Topal

Volunteers

Susan Abraham
Sylvia Anderson
Jim Arth
Penelope Arth
Eleanor Bauer
Robert Boggs
Stephanie Bowlson
Ali Cavanaugh
Susan Clough
Madelin Coit
Eduardo Difarnecio
Carolyn Eason
Maryt Fredrickson
Jane Gaziano
Benji Geary
Marie Gee
Kathy and Jim Gentry
Roger Griffith
Robin Guido
Kirk Haines
David Hershey
Mija Hübler
Judy Just
Alan Karp
Shirley and Fred Klinghoffer
Jay Kobrin
Denise Kusel
Katrina Lasko
Susan Latham
David Margolis
Elizabeth Martin
Barbara McIntyre
Gordon Micunis
Patt & Norman Millett
Carolyn Mills
Jean Moss
Susan Munroe
Hannah Nawmann
Peter Prandoni

Jane Reid
Leslie Rich
Lynda Rodolitz
Jennifer Royster
Heidi Rudisch
John Tatone
Gretchen Thies
Tina Turner
Christine Wendel
Sarah Williams
Ray Wittenberg
Natasha Yates
Peter Zavadil

Gallery Attendants

Meredy Baldridge
Jamison Dancing Eagle
Mary Lynn Dodson
Lali Flores
Robert Hernandez
Bill Hinsvark
Max Ludington
Amy Mattison
Norma Ortega
Nicole Ringer
Jennifer Sullivan

All photography by Herbert Lotz unless noted below.

page 1
Computer rendering by Graft Design

pages 2-3
Jennifer Schlesinger

pages 22-23
Courtesy of Michael Werner, Inc.,
New York, New York

page 26
Nic Tenwiggenhorn

page 27
Courtesy of Karsten Schubert,
London, England

pages 50-51
Robert Reck

pages 54-55
Jeff Burton

pages 60-63
Video stills by Norma Ortega

page 67
Jessica Stockholder

pages 68-69
Carole Devillers

pages 82-83
Kenneth Anger
(stills by Michael Friend)

pages 86-87
Jeff Burton

pages 88-89
Courtesy of Michael Werner, Inc.,
New York, New York

pages 90-91
Nic Tenwiggenhorn

pages 94-95
Computer renderings by Graft Design

page 96
Robert Wedemeyer

pages 100-101
Computer diagrams by Jim Isermann

pages 102-103
Courtesy of Matthew Marks Gallery,
New York, New York

pages 104-105
Robert Reck

pages 108-109
Courtesy of Jay Jopling/White Cube,
London, England

pages 110-111
Computer drawings by Takashi
Murakami and Hiropon Factory

pages 112-113
Stills by Nic Nicosia

pages 114-115
Thomas R. DuBrock

pages 116-117
Computer renderings by Jorge Pardo

pages 120-121
Stills by Stephen Prina

pages 122-123
Courtesy of Karsten Schubert,
London, England

pages 124-125
Ed Ruscha
(stills by Michael Friend)

pages 128-129
Andre Morain. Courtesy of Riva
Yares Gallery, Santa Fe, New Mexico
and Scottsdale, Arizona

pages 134-135
Courtesy of Lisson Gallery
London, England

This catalogue has been published
on the occasion of S I T E Santa Fe's
Fourth International Biennial,
*Beau Monde: Toward a
Redeemed Cosmopolitanism*
(July 14, 2001 — January 6, 2002).

ISBN: 0-9700774-5-9

© 2002 SITE Santa Fe

1606 Paseo de Peralta
Santa Fe, New Mexico 87501
tel 505 989-1199
fax 505 989-1188
www.sitesantafe.org

Editing and
Catalogue Production:
Rebecca Friedman

Design:
Twelvetrees Publishers
Jack Woody
Arlyn Eve Nathan

Typefaces:
Minion, Frutiger, and Poetica

Printed and Bound:
Seoul, South Korea